Fundamentals of Disability Inclusion

Unveiling Stereotypes, Unleashing Opportunities

By Linda Fitzpatrick

DEDICATION

For my Mom Katy, whose indomitable spirit shines on.

Table of Contents

INTRODUCTION

"We don't see things as they are; we see things as we are."
The Talmud

Technological, medical and legislative breakthroughs have changed the game for people with disability. Every thoughtful individual and organization strives to rise above the stereotypes and biases of the old days to become culturally competent with people of all abilities. This engaging book will put you well on the way to a new realm of consciousness and sensitivity:

- Learn the culture and needs of people with different disabilities: hearing, vision, mobility, non-apparent disabilities (like learning disabilities, mental health issues, autism) as well as the needs of people who have had the recent onset of a disability;
- Learn tools and techniques for many settings: in stressful situations; when important instructions must be followed; when conflict arises; when communications challenges occur;
- Develop greater confidence and competence when you encounter disability among family, friends, co-workers or anywhere.

This book is designed for anyone who feels called to a new level of disability competence. It's for those in academia and business, lawyers and teachers, coaches, ministers, restaurant wait staff and more. Be prepared to be surprised, informed and empowered in this important realm.

My mom had difficulty walking in her 20s when I was just a child, and the Rheumatoid Arthritis that caused her pain and inflammation progressed through her life, the damage to her vascular system resulting in an amputated leg. When we were out for dinner it was common for the wait-person, noticing her wheelchair, to ask me: *"Will she have fries with that burger?"* I cringed for her. *"Ask her"* I would respond as my own awareness and response to limiting attitudes began to emerge.

Today there is a world of opportunity for people with disability. But the shadow side – limiting attitudes and beliefs – hasn't caught up with what's possible. My hope is that this book will help us root out the prejudice and shine light on the opportunities.

Linda Fitzpatrick

EXPANDING AWARENESS

You can observe a lot by watching.

Yogi Berra

Let's consider some different situations and how you might respond.

Imagine you're out running errands and as you climb some steps you notice a woman in front of you who seems to be struggling with her packages. You wonder if she's injured, or if she has a medical condition. Should you help her with the packages or pass her by?

Or imagine you're at a meeting, and one of the participants has a stutter - should you help him by finishing his sentence?

Or, you're walking on the street and you notice a blind woman approaching using her mobility cane to detect obstacles but she's clearly unaware of an overhanging sign that she's about to collide with. What should you do?

Like many people, you're probably not sure what to do in any of these instances.

What if when you try to help the woman struggling with her packages, she is offended and rebuffs your offer? But if you just walk by, are you being insensitive?

If you help the man with a stutter to finish his sentence, you might guess his meaning incorrectly, making things worse. But if you wait for him to finish, the awkwardness of watching him struggle to speak can make everyone uncomfortable.

And the blind woman? She's about to smack her head into that sign and in that moment, you hesitate about whether or not to warn her . . . bang!

Sometimes what to do isn't so obvious, so let's have a look at these different situations.

The Woman with The Packages: Honoring Independence versus Being Helpful

In our interactions with people we routinely, and often unconsciously, navigate priorities as we choose what to say and do. When you notice a stranger struggling with packages, is your priority to respect her privacy and independence or is your priority the honorable urge to help out? Later we'll talk more about specific principles to keep in mind, but in this case the principle that might apply is "Ask Before Helping". If you were to approach the woman - without startling her - and gain her attention with full eye contact, she may give you a visual clue as to whether she would welcome your help or not. Maybe her body language would suggest *"butt out*!" If it isn't clear, you could offer, "*May I give you a hand with those bags?*"

Even if the woman accepts your kind offer, there is more to consider. Stay in the conversation with her. Let her guide you. Ask her if she wants the packages at the top of the step, or inside. Find out if she would like you to support her arm or not.

Navigate those competing priorities - watchfulness for her well-being and respect for her independence and privacy - by asking questions. There's no right or wrong answer for the two of you. It's your chance for a moment's gracious interaction with another person. Everybody wins.

The Man Who Stutters: Patience and The Pregnant Silence

A person with a stutter or another kind of speech impediment may need a bit of time to make his thoughts known. The best thing for the listener to do is wait. Take a deep, calming breath if you need to, but just wait.

This waiting can create the dreaded "pregnant silence" hanging in the air. It's the silence filled with people wondering "*Will this ever end...?*" Onlookers can become jittery and self-conscious, embarrassed to be witnessing the person's struggles and assuming the person is as uncomfortable as they are, which may not be true. Chances are the person with the stutter has learned to adapt to his own and other's reactions.

Slow down and wait. Tolerate a little silence. You may be surprised to notice that your capacity to listen is actually expanding.

The Woman Who Is Blind: Safety Trumps All

My friend and colleague Betty Bird became blind when, at the age of seven, she was struck by a baseball. Betty went on to enjoy a successful career including a stint as Senior Vice President for Rehabilitation at New York Lighthouse Vision Rehabilitation Services. In that position Dr. Bird directed 45 rehabilitation programs for people with impaired vision and administered a budget of $16 Million.

Consider Betty's single most important piece of advice for being with someone who is blind. Talk. Just talk. Say what you see. Say what you want. Say what you think she might want. Just talk.

People who meet Betty for the first time typically are a bit nervous. They are afraid to say or do the wrong thing. Like many of us when encountering the unfamiliar, they question their instincts. They walk on eggshells.

Thinking again about the blind woman heading into the overhang, let's decide to speak up. If you need to shout a warning to keep someone from walking into an overhang – or walking off a cliff -- just shout or grab the person to safety, for safety's sake!

Walgreen's, America's largest drug-store chain, has a commitment to integrate people with disability throughout its workforce. There's a sign painted on the wall of its first inclusive distribution center: the word 'them' in a circle, with a cross through it. Randy Lewis, former Senior Vice President, said *"There is no them. Once you see a person with a disability as you, not them, other things fade away. You might still see the differences but those are minor compared to how we are all alike."*

WHAT IS DISABILITY?

May your trails be crooked, winding, lonesome, dangerous,
leading to the most amazing view.

Edward Abbey

Taking a defining phrase from the 2013 revision of the Americans with Disabilities Act (The ADA): A disability is a physical or mental impairment that substantially limits one or more major life activity.[i]

This is an extremely broad definition of disability. If you had a head cold and you had difficulty concentrating at work, you would have a disability under this definition, wouldn't you? That impairment of your breathing, the distractions of sneezing, pain and muscle aches, might limit your ability to do your work. That head cold might qualify as a disability under the ADA definition.

The ADA when it was initially signed by President Bush in 1990 had a much more narrow definition of disability but it was so narrow that anyone with a disability had great difficulty proving discrimination under this law. So the language of the law was greatly broadened in the Amendments (ADA Amendments Act of 2008)[ii].

There are different definitions of disability depending on the intent. A person who seeks government assistance from the Social Security administration will need proof under a more stringent definition of disability.

The US Census makes a distinction between disability and "severe" disability in their population counts and tracking to assist development of policies and to guide allocation of taxpayer funded resources.

For many of us the first thing that comes to mind when we think of disability is the wheelchair since the wheelchair user is the icon for disability in our society.

However, wheelchair users represent just a tiny fraction of the population of people with disabilities. The scope and range of disability, discussed further in a later chapter, includes:

- Mobility issues
- Hearing
- Speech
- Vision
- Non-Apparent Disabilities including Mental Health issues

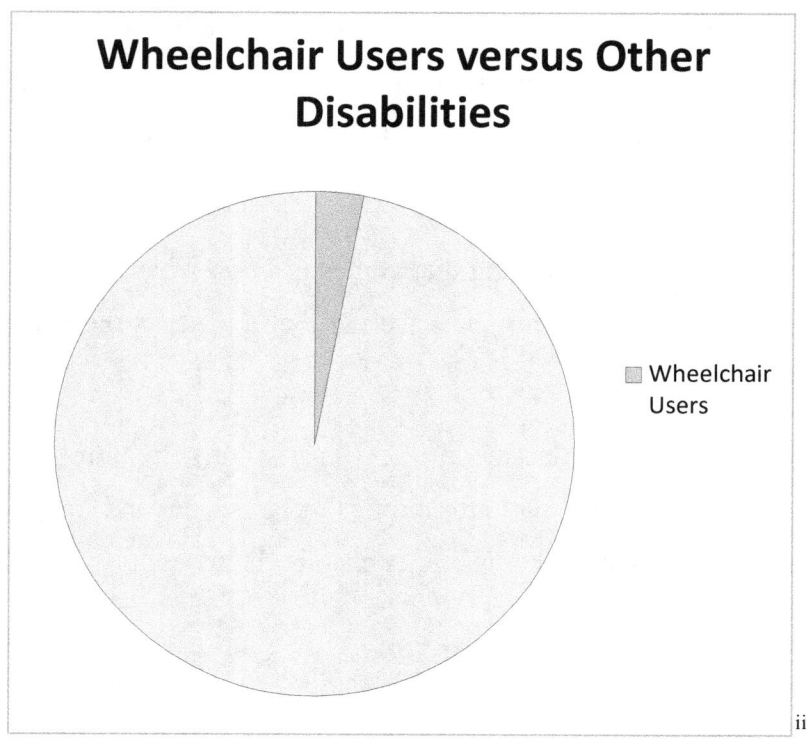

Wheelchair Users versus Other Disabilities

Wheelchair Users

iii

In addition to the breadth of how disability occurs, it can also be of short or long duration. It can be progressive and get worse. It can be reversed and get better through medical intervention.

Two people with the same disability diagnosis can have vastly different experiences depending on matters of temperament – adaptability for example – and on context – for example, how much access the person has to adaptive equipment and supportive people.

For our purposes, disability has to do with "substantial limitation", the phrase used in the ADA. And who among us doesn't have substantial limitation in one realm or another?

Variation in ability is ordinary, not special. "Substantial limitation" of one kind or another affects most of us for at least part of our lives.

A TSUNAMI IN OUR CULTURE

When I was young, disabilities of all sorts were governed by a code of silence. You didn't speak about them outside the family.

Sonia Sotomayor, U.S. Supreme Court Associate Justice (diagnosed with diabetes as a child)

A Tsunami in Attitudes

There has been a tsunami - a great wave of change - about disability in recent decades.

Sonia Sotomayor was appointed an Associate Justice of the Supreme Court of the United States. In her book <u>My Beloved World</u>^{iv} Sotomayor described what it was like to grow up as a child with a disability. When she was seven years old she was diagnosed with juvenile onset diabetes. Sotomayor is insulin dependent. She has to test her blood and adjust her insulin several times a day every day. The serious health risks of diabetes include cardiovascular and neurological complications.

Even with a serious medical diagnosis Justice Sotomayor leads a life of extraordinary accomplishment. Yet as the quote above suggests, when she was a child her disability was the subject of shame.

During his Presidency from 1933 until 1945, President Franklin Delano Roosevelt achieved many accomplishments including leading the United States to victory during World War II. FDR became one of the most beloved of US Presidents but most Americans never knew he was a wheelchair user. The Press Corps wouldn't photograph him in his wheelchair,

From an article entitled "Living Well with Down Syndrome" by Post Columnist George Will with his son Jon, daughter Victoria and son Geoff

which he used following a bout of Polio that left him partially paralyzed years before his Presidency. They hid from view a critical part of who he was in a well-intentioned gesture to protect him from the unbridled disability prejudice of the era.

Columnist George Will's son Jon was born with Down syndrome in 1972. The day after Jon was born, a doctor's first question for Jon's parents was whether they intended to take Jon home from the hospital. [v] That would be unheard of today.

Today, there are summer camps where kids with juvenile onset diabetes can stretch and play and learn while getting the medical supervision they need. This was unheard of when Supreme Court Justice Sonia Sotomayor was a child.

Today it seems unthinkable that a leader's wheelchair would be deliberately hidden from view by the Press Corps.

And a child with Down syndrome has the possibility of education, employment and a full range of choices far beyond what would be available in an institutionalized life.

A Tsunami of Prevalence

Almost one in five Americans has a disability and about two thirds of that number have a "severe" disability defined by the US Census as needing assistance with one or more activities of daily living.vi

The prevalence of disability is increasing partly because of medical advances. Cancer treatment options have continued to expand preserving life but, in some cases, leaving the cancer survivor with a disability. For example, a cancer in the occipital lobe of the brain that would have been deadly years ago can now be treated successfully. However, the treatment could result in significant vision loss for the patient.

A car crash that would have killed now leaves someone alive, but with a neurological impairment.

Soldiers who would have died on the battlefield just ten years ago are now saved – though they may have amputated limbs.

Our population is aging. The prevalence of disability increases dramatically with the years. People in the oldest age group measured by Census – people 80 years or older – were about 8 times as likely to have a disability as people in the youngest age group.

The so-called Baby Boomer generation – people born after the end of World War II – is redefining aging with their continued representation in the workplace as well as in active leisure activities. These folks are moving through their sixties, seventies, eighties and beyond with active, vibrant lifestyles while accommodating disabilities like arthritis with hip replacements and knee replacements and exercise regimens, pursuing glaucoma surgeries and other treatments and wellness protocols that permit them to move beyond constraints of disability.

The prevalence of disability will continue to impact our communities at work, at play, at worship, when we travel and when we shop. Disability confidence is important for any socially competent person and is increasingly required to be business as usual in our commercial enterprises.

FACILITATING RELATIONSHIPS: SEVEN THEMES

Clearly, the community of people with disability is very large and very diverse. Throughout this book we'll familiarize you with the culture and accommodation needs of many different types of disability. But knowing what someone's diagnosis is should not dictate what you choose to do or not do. One person who uses a wheelchair may need help transferring from the wheelchair into the car. Another person with the very same medical diagnosis, who is the same gender and similar in age and weight and apparent strength, may not need assistance.

One person who is blind may be a Braille reader, another may not read Braille at all.

1. Ask before helping.
2. Maintain eye contact.
3. Don't shout.
4. Avoid outdated language.
5. Don't worry about reminding someone of her disability.
6. Don't pretend to understand if you don't.
7. See the person first, not the disability.

One person who is deaf may be a proficient lip reader, another may not have much proficiency with that at all but might have mastered technological adaptations.

Our personal attributes and characteristics affect how we adapt in the world. Some people are shy and sensitive. Some people are assertive and thick-skinned.

Therefore, in this section we present some fundamental guidelines to inform you across many different circumstances.

> Please don't touch a person's wheelchair without permission.

It's important to tell you that there are very few hard and fast rules.

Apply your good judgment to these guidelines and your disability confidence will become much stronger.

#1 Ask Before Helping

At the University of Illinois Tatyana McFadden's teammates on the school's wheelchair racing team have nicknamed her Beast. Why? Because Tatyana is strong. In the gym people stop and gawk at how much she is lifting. In a road race spectators marvel at how she flies up hills that bring other racers to a crawl. On the track her competitors hang their heads as they see Tatyana's rippling shoulders cross the finish line ahead of them. Tatyana is strong as a beast.

When Tatyana hears the nickname, however, she giggles. Being strong is not something Tatyana has ever had to think about, it is something that she has embodied her whole life.

Not everyone who has a disability becomes a Paralympic athlete, that's for sure. But most everyone has gained the mastery they need to succeed in the world.

Wheelchair users tell us how common it is to be pushed by a well-intended stranger. It's startling, unexpected, and an invasion of physical space.

My blind friend Betty Bird explains her aversion to unwanted help:

"It's unbelievable how people treat me sometimes. People grab me physically to try to plop me into a chair, or they manhandle me to get me through a doorway. I'm not deaf. I'm blind. Just tell me where the door is for heaven's sake!"

Sometimes people can be overly solicitous. Pat returned to work following an extended absence that included cancer surgery. Her co-workers had difficulty relating to Pat in the same way they did before her absence. People were tentative around her, overly protective. Well-meaning but inappropriate. Pat was fit for duty. If she needed help she would ask for it.

Whatever it is that interferes with your interaction, chances are you won't guess your way to effective communication. Don't be afraid to ask the person what will help. You can expect that this conversation will be productive for both of you, and certainly more productive than guessing.

#2 Maintain Eye Contact

"The question is not what you look at, but what you see."
Henry David Thoreau

In this fast-paced world it's amazing how often we break eye contact when we're in conversation. Our attention is diverted from our co-workers, our spouses, our children. We're only "half-listening". Our minds are racing ahead to the next task, the next obligation, the next place we need to be. Our eyes are diverted. That's a clue that we're not really paying attention.

Adults make eye contact between 30% and 60% of the time in an average conversation, says the communications-analytics company Quantified Impressions. But the Austin, Texas, company says people should be making eye contact 60% to 70% of the time to create a sense of emotional connection, according to its analysis of 3,000 people speaking to individuals and groups.

When we are in conversation with a person who has a disability, the commonplace habit - breaking eye contact - can be an even more serious impediment to rapport and communication.

When you're speaking with a person in a wheelchair for more than a few minutes, either sit or bend so that you can see eye-to-eye.

When you're conversing with a person who is blind, let the person know if you are breaking eye contact to reach for something. Otherwise, she'll continue chatting away as though you were there – and she may be embarrassed at the discovery.

Avoid startling any person by coming up from behind. A person who is hearing, visually or cognitively impaired may be particularly vulnerable because she lacks the cues that you are approaching.

- A hearing person will detect your footfall whereas someone who doesn't hear or doesn't hear well won't detect that.

- A person who is blind may not have peripheral vision to spot your approach.
- Someone with a neurological condition may have trouble re-shifting focus.

It's perfectly okay to get someone's attention by tapping her shoulder or waving a hand. Just remember that the tapping must be gentle – too often our brethren with disabilities complain of being touched or moved roughly.

> The impact of eye contact is so powerful because it is instinctive and connected with humans' early survival patterns. Children who could attract and maintain eye contact, and therefore increase attention, had the best chance of being fed and cared for.

In conversation with a person who is hearing impaired, it's important for him to have an unobstructed view of your lips as you are speaking. Sustained eye contact is the best way to maintain the face-to-face orientation.

Good eye contact lets you stay tuned in to the other person's emotional state. If you're working with someone or explaining something, you will be able to note anxiety or confusion in their eyes. The sooner you notice this the sooner you can address it: *"Shall I go over that again?"* or *"Would you like me to show you a picture to illustrate what I mean?"*

Remember that appropriate eye contact is an investment in attentiveness. It will help you stay engaged, relaxed and focused on the other person.

A common and heartfelt complaint among some people with disabilities is "feeling invisible". A person who has cerebral palsy may have an uneven gait, slurred speech or an odd demeanor. Passersby may avert their eyes and ignore her because of their own discomfiture. A person in a wheelchair who travels with a walking companion will often be ignored. The simple reminder to maintain eye contact can improve the quality of all of your relationships.

#3 Don't Shout

Our third theme – don't shout – is something we might try to remember all the time: when we speak with our co-workers, friends, family... even our dogs! But for some reason as soon as we aren't understood, we shout! WE ALL DO IT!!! Ooops.

Of course, we know that shouting produces anxiety – both for us and for the person who has to listen to us. And yet our friends and colleagues with disabilities tell us that being shouted at is commonplace. People in wheelchairs are shouted at. People who are blind are shouted at. People who don't understand because of a cognitive disorder are shouted at. People with hearing impairments are shouted at. But wait - wouldn't that work? To shout at someone who has a hearing impairment so they could hear the louder voice?

No. Shouting does not make it easier to hear if a person uses a hearing aid, or has a cochlear implant or is deaf. In fact,

> Microphones are just like people. If you shout at them they get scared.
>
> -Beatle Paul McCartney

shouting may produce a more garbled sound than speaking in a normal tone of voice. Shouting also creates undue and unwanted attention. It can be embarrassing for all parties.

Instead of shouting, it is more helpful to slow down, speak clearly, and try to get to a quiet place without distractions and to pay close attention.

Once again, a simple theme to keep in mind – DON'T SHOUT! Hmmm. Don't shout.

#4 Avoid Outdated Language

This theme may be a little bit trickier than some of the others because it may not be so easy to know what is outdated. We try to avoid the word "handicapped" because its genesis harkens back to the days when a person with a disability begged for change in his cap. Yet all over the United States we have parking spaces designated "handicapped" that provide important access for those who need it.

People who live with an intellectual, or developmental disability, in most cases, are no longer referred to as "retarded".

Nevertheless, a Mom who has an adult child with Down syndrome may refer to him as "retarded" because it is a holdover from his youth when he attended special programs for "retarded children". We certainly would not correct her language.

Generally speaking, we believe that an open and inclusive intention is the most important thing. A compassionate and caring heart will convey a more accurate and clearer meaning than a proper phrase accompanied by an uncaring attitude.

Jill Bolte Taylor, brain scientist and author of the stunning memoir Stroke of Insight[vii] writes: *"Don't bother asking me yes or no questions as a stroke victim because I don't know what yes or no means. Ask multiple choice and be present, be conscious to my responses. If I'm just the next thing on your busy schedule then why bother."*

The guidelines on the following page have been provided by our friends at the National Business & Disability Council:

Words with Dignity	Avoid these Words
Person with a disability	Crippled/handicapped/invalid
Person who has/person with (e.g., person who has cerebral palsy)	Victim/afflicted with/suffers with (e.g. victim of cerebral palsy)
Wheelchair user	Restricted, confined to a wheelchair/wheelchair bound
Deaf/does not voice for themselves/nonvocal	Deaf mute/deaf and dumb
Disabled since birth/born with	Birth defect
Psychiatric history/psychiatric disability/emotional disorder/mental illness	Crazy/insane/ mental patient
Epilepsy/seizures	Fits
Learning disability/mental developmental disability	Slow, retarded, lazy, stupid, underachiever

#5 Don't Worry About Reminding Someone of their Disability

It's not in anyone's best interest for typically abled people to be "walking on eggshells" around people who have disabilities. By "walking on eggshells" we refer to the feeling that no matter what we say or do it will be wrong.

> The University's Master's program has two students with the same name so they're distinguished as blind Josh and sighted Josh. This illustrates the relaxed attitude and lack of self-consciousness that marks an inclusive environment.

If we're talking with someone who is blind and we say, *"I see what you mean!"* we can might feel embarrassed at what we've just implied – that they can "see". But, of course, it's a fair question. What you're asking is *"Do you get my point?"*

If we're talking with someone who is deaf and we say *"I hear you!"* isn't that, in the same vein, an appropriate confirmation that you *"get the point"*. Don't worry about reminding someone of their disability. They know.

People who are deaf, or blind, or in wheelchairs or who have other disabilities have lived in the world for a long time. They know how to get around, to get what they need. They know how to be happy. At any given moment that person may be happier than you are. Or sadder. Or more fulfilled. Or less fulfilled.

Don't worry about reminding someone of his disability. Relax. Stop worrying. Get to know him and what he needs. Pay attention to her.

Connect with your compassionate nature – toward yourself and everyone around you.

#6 Don't Pretend To Understand If You Don't

When we don't understand one another, it can be frustrating. It can cause anxiety and can tempt us to simply pretend to understand, even when we don't. This pretending can lead to more serious problems rooted in incorrect understanding. Make up your mind that you will stick with the communication until you both find a way to understand one another. It will be worth the commitment.

Jane, 26, is a successful marketing director who has amassed sizable savings which she wants to invest. She meets with her financial advisor, George, in order to create an investment strategy which will enable her to buy the home of her dreams by the time she is 35. Jane's advisor does not understand that she has a learning disability called Dyscalculia, a math disability which can interfere with a person's ability to understand computations. When George explains some of his preliminary ideas for financial products he fails to notice Jane's eyes glaze over. She asks some preliminary questions but it is clear he's not hearing her confusion. As a result, Jane decides to work with a different financial advisor who listens more closely and is more patient and skillful. George remains baffled about why he lost this client.

A hearing-impaired man is injured in a motor vehicle accident and is rushed to the Emergency Room where a history is taken, including information about medications and allergies. In this noisy setting it is very difficult for the patient to understand the questions thrown at him so he answers in a perfunctory way. As a result, much of the information he has given is incorrect and he is in real jeopardy.

A person's ability to correctly understand and communicate may be compromised for many reasons: due to a hearing or a cognitive disorder, a learning disability, being on the Autism spectrum or being stressed and anxious. That is why it is so important to slow down, listen carefully, manage your own anxiety and employ effective communication strategies.

One effective technique is to check what you've heard by asking: *"Let me say it back to you, tell me if I've got it right."* Then wait, let the person collect her thoughts and respond. Your role is to listen carefully and correct any miscommunication until you completely understand. Don't panic if you don't understand right away. Deep listening is profoundly respectful and may be the single quickest way to build trust and rapport.

Most importantly, don't pretend to understand if you don't. There can be any number of negative consequences as a result.

#7 See the Person First, Not the Disability

RoseAnn Ashby, a Branch Chief at the U.S. Department of Education reports *"I am blind and use a computer equipped with a screen reader with speech output to enable me to review and edit the work of my staff."* Jonathan Parker is legally deaf, but oversees large sums of money as a Fund Accountant for a Portland, Maine financial services firm. Jenni Gold, who was diagnosed with muscular dystrophy at six months-old, is a member of the Director's Guild of America, and Chief Executive Officer of her own independent company. (reference by the US info.state.gov) People with disabilities are people first. Some people with disabilities are kind and well-mannered. Some are crusty and cranky. Some are smart and curious. Some are lackadaisical. Some are ambitious.

When my mother had a leg amputated due to complications of RA - Rheumatoid Arthritis –we went to Staten Island University Hospital to a support group to learn more about adapting to her prosthesis.

That room full of forty or so people represented people who had lost one leg, two legs, one arm, both arms. Here were young people, elderly people, hopeful people, funny people, grumpy people, bored people; just the same spread of types I'd find anywhere. It made such an impression on me. My mother went on to live many vibrant years in her wheelchair due to her tenacity and love of life.

"Disability" is just one small part of who a person is.

If you're in a health care facility, law office, or other organization that serves the public, or if you work at a theme park or a retail store, you can post these simple themes in the staff area as an easy reminder.

Disability Inclusion - Seven Themes

1. Ask before helping.
2. Maintain eye contact.
3. Don't Shout.
4. Avoid outdated language.
5. Don't worry about reminding someone of their disability.
6. Don't pretend to understand if you don't.
7. See the person first, not the disability.

CULTURE OF DIFFERENT DISABILITIES

"The impeded stream is the one that sings."
From The Real Work by Wendell Berry

This chapter will provide you with a sense of the wide range of disabilities that people live with. Begin to notice, in your own circle of friends, family and coworkers, the diversity and accommodation that marks successful living. Read on to become more respectful about what different people manage in their extraordinary and ordinary lives.

Mobility Issues

Usually when we think of mobility issues, a wheelchair comes to mind. Yet many people have mobility challenges without using a wheelchair. A person may use crutches or a walker, or use leg braces. He may move slowly or need to walk with assistance. She may only use a wheelchair part of the time in her

John Little, Founder & CEO of the Successful Resumes Global Consultancy and father of beautiful bride Vicky

strategy to conserve energy. Mobility issues may stem from injury, accident or disease. They may be permanent (a spinal cord injury), progressive (Muscular Dystrophy) or temporary (a broken leg following a sports accident).

Mobility issues may also combine with other challenges. Someone with RA (Rheumatoid Arthritis) is apt to experience chronic pain which can interfere with concentration. This means the person not only has difficulty walking but may also encounter communication problems. Someone with a spinal cord injury may experience respiratory,  circulatory and bladder problems which can complicate travel. Someone who has a temporary sports injury may lack proficiency with his crutches.

People learn to adapt. They continue to engage in work and play, in worship and vacation. They have accommodated their particular requirements as much as possible.

Someone who is moving slowly due to mobility impairment may simply need your patience. She might become anxious if you try to "help her along". You may feel the urge to open a door for her. Ask her first so that your well-meant gesture doesn't unknowingly cause her to feel tense and rushed.

There are some special considerations for a wheelchair user that may open up your thinking about your interactions with people in general:

- Never touch a person's wheelchair, cane, crutch or any other assistive device without permission. Consider that these are part of the individual's personal space.

- Don't push a person's wheelchair without permission. If you try to help someone over a curb without waiting for instructions, you may inadvertently tip the person out of the chair.

- Don't impose on a wheelchair user to carry things like coats or packages. You'd be amazed how often this happens.

- The wheelchair user may appreciate your alerting him to the most accessible route within your office complex, or where accessible bathrooms are located.

- Handle a person's wheelchair as a critical precision instrument and follow the direction of the user. If leg rests are to be removed be sure to find out exactly how to remove them. If the chair is to be stowed in a car's trunk be sure there is ample room for stowage and that the chair is secured. A damaged wheelchair can be extremely dangerous for the rider.

- If the wheelchair user is going to transfer (moving to a chair or into a car) be sure you follow her specific instructions. Some people are capable of lifting themselves out of the wheelchair whereas others need assistance. Many unnecessary injuries occur during transfer because a helper rushes, doesn't listen, or doesn't comply with a request.

In her illuminating book <u>The Question of David: A Disabled Mother's Journey Through Adoption, Family, and Life</u> Denise Sherer Jacobson[viii] describes her experience as a frequent airline traveler in a wheelchair. She came to expect that airline staff would handle her just like they would any baggage. Even though she is perfectly capable of transferring herself and can do so more efficiently than being carried by someone else, Denise seldom is given the opportunity to say so.

And Denise's challenge is compounded because she has a speech impairment. Rushed and preoccupied, most airline staff folks don't take their time to listen. After all her years of flying, she still knows that *"they'd rather lift than communicate."*

Ask a person what he or she needs. Listen, wait and accommodate.

<u>Hearing/Speech Issues</u>

Like mobility issues, hearing issues exist on a continuum. At one end of the spectrum are the people who have been born deaf -- who have never experienced speech and sound the way hearing people have. At the other end is the person who is just beginning to experience hearing loss due to age or a disease and who hasn't developed adaptive strategies yet.

When communicating with a person who has a hearing deficit, speak slowly (or at least not too quickly) and find a distraction-free environment to the extent that is possible. Maintain eye contact and be sure you have the person's attention before you begin speaking. Of course, these principles apply to all of our conversations, don't they? Yet so often we are distracted.

People who are deaf communicate in various ways. They may be proficient in reading lips or they may not. They may be proficient in American Sign Language (ASL), which is an entirely different language from English, with a syntax all its own.

The culture of the deaf community is unique in that it is one of the most actively engaged in advocacy within the world of people with disabilities. Gallaudet University, the world's only university to offer programs and services are specifically designed to accommodate deaf and

> Deaf people can do anything except hear.
> -Marlee Maitlin, Oscar winning actress who is deaf.

hard of hearing students, was founded in 1864 by an Act of Congress, and its charter was signed by President Abraham Lincoln. Gallaudet has more than 20,000 alumni around the world.

Marlee Matlin is a deaf actress who received worldwide critical acclaim for her film debut in Paramount Pictures' "Children of a Lesser God". At 21, she became the youngest recipient of the Best Actress Oscar and only one of four actresses to receive the honor for her film debut.

In 2013, Marlee appeared in a landmark episode of the TV drama "Switched at Birth", an ABC family original series, where the segment is silent, entirely in American Sign Language.

The Switched at Birth episode is based on a true story. Gallaudet University students protested because they wanted the president of the university, who had always been a person who could hear, to be deaf. After a week of protests, the students got their wish in a new, deaf president.

Another well-known groundbreaker, Helen Keller, became an international celebrity who taught the world to respect people who are blind and deaf. Her mission evolved from her own life. When Helen was nine months old she became ill with what may have been meningitis causing her to lose both vision and hearing. Her story inspired William Gibson's play and award-winning film, "The Miracle Worker," about Helen's lifelong relationship with Anne Sullivan, the tutor who taught her to communicate.

If you are to be in conversation with someone who is deaf or hard of hearing here are some things to keep in mind:

- Seek a quiet, distraction-free space for conversation.
- Have ready access to writing implements and a comfortable place to write.
- If you have trouble understanding, let the person know.
- Be flexible. Try using another word, hand gestures, or writing.

- Avoid eating, drinking, chewing gum, or obscuring your mouth with your hand while speaking.

- Someone with a hearing loss may speak louder than necessary. Avoid misinterpreting the person's volume as aggression. It's perfectly okay to ask the person to lower her voice if that would be appropriate. If your request is accompanied by a smile, all the better.

- Someone may be deaf or hard of hearing in only one ear. The person may tell you, you may notice only one hearing aid, or you can ask if he or she has better hearing in one ear than the other. It would then be easy to position yourself on that side.

Cochlear implants are becoming more common. A cochlear implant is surgically implanted under the ear of a person with a profound hearing impairment in order to make sounds clearer. The implant does not create the same hearing as for a person without a hearing impairment, but it does allow the person with the implant to interpret sounds.

> The public must learn that the blind man is neither genius nor a freak nor an idiot. He has a mind that can be educated, a hand which can be trained, and ambitions which it is right for him to strive to realize, and it is the duty of the public to help him make the best of himself so that he can win light through work. - Helen Keller

If a person with a hearing impairment uses sign language and has an interpreter, speak directly to the hearing-impaired individual. The interpreter is there to facilitate the conversation.

If you become more aware, you may come to realize that you can improve your relationships simply by paying attention to how people hear.

Vision Issues

Visual impairments also occur on a continuum. A person may be blind – able to see only shadows and movement – or legally blind -- able to see shapes and some details. A person may have a diagnosis of Macular Degeneration which will reduce visual acuity and may interfere with central vision. A person who lacks depth perception has difficulty perceiving how far away things are and as a result may be at greater risk of falling, especially when going down stairs. A person may be color blind: *"turn right when you see the red barn"* is no help.

As you get to know someone who has a vision impairment you'll quickly learn any necessary adaptations with disability competence you've mastered.

Dr. Betty Bird, the retired Senior VP we met previously, lives in the Adirondacks where she keeps and cares for two beautiful horses. Dr. Bird emphasizes the advice to sighted people. Talk about what you need her to do. Talk about what you expect. Talk about what you see. If you are guiding a person who is blind through a room, tell her what the room looks like especially in terms of where doors, seats and other objects may be positioned. Be specific about any potential obstacles such as stairs, a crack in the sidewalk, wet floors, objects protruding from the wall and so forth. For example, saying *"Be careful, there is an opened filing cabinet in front of you."* is better than simply saying *"Look out."* When you give instructions, make them specific.

For example, say, *"Walk forward to the end of this aisle and make a full right"* rather than saying *"Make a right when you reach the furniture department"*. The person may not know where the furniture department is. Offer to read any necessary written information, such as menus, agendas or instructions. If you are exchanging money, count out change so that the person knows which bills are which.

If you are inviting a blind person to be seated, tap the seat so she can hear where it is. If you offer a cold drink, you might ask to take the person's hand and guide it to where the cold drink is placed on a table. Show where the end of the table  is by tapping it. Keep the person informed. Tell him where you are and what you're doing. ..."*I'm going behind a desk to get a form.*"

Remember to speak directly to the person, not her companion. It's all too common for the blind person to hear her companion addressed: *"Does she have a ticket?"* Imagine how disrespectful that feels. Never touch a person who is blind before asking permission. Ask *"May I take your hand?"* Or *"Would you like to take my arm?"*

A Word about Service Animals

When we think of a "service animal" we might be most apt to think of a "seeing-eye dog" or "guide dog" which assists a person who is blind. You may be surprised to learn that many animals other than dogs provide service to people with disabilities and that a wide range of disabilities can be served through our helpers from the animal world.

A person who is deaf might have a hearing cat to make him aware of noises around him. The Service Animal Registry of America (SARA)[ix] registers and certifies service and therapy dogs, cats, monkeys, birds, horses and more.

Service animals may:

- Assist a person who is blind;
- Alert a person with a hearing impairment to sounds such as a doorbell, an alarm clock or smoke alarm, a knock at the door or even the cry of a baby;
- Pull a wheelchair user or carry or pick things up for a person with a mobility impairment;

- Alert a person with a seizure disorder to the onset of the seizure or someone with diabetes to a drop in blood sugar;
- Provide emotional and other support to a person who has Autism by providing a focal point or helping to divert thoughts;
- Reminding a person with mental illness to take prescribed medication;
- Serve on "facility teams" working with adults who are rehabilitation professionals or educators, helping to improve the mental, physical or emotional health of those in their care.

According to Canine Companions for Independence, their team working at a physical therapy center might engage patients in simple therapy exercises such as throwing a ball for the dog to retrieve. A team working at a program for people with developmental disabilities might focus on scheduled activities such as feeding time for the dog or grooming. Such experiences can be helpful in broadening daily living skills.

Laws about Service Animals

Under the ADA, State and local governments, businesses, and nonprofit organizations that serve the public generally must allow service animals to accompany people with disabilities in all areas of the facility where the public is normally allowed to go.

According to the Department of Justice, when it is not obvious what service an animal provides, only limited inquiries are allowed. Staff may ask two questions: (1) is the dog a service animal required because of a disability, and (2) what work or task has the dog been trained to perform. Staff cannot ask about the person's disability, require medical documentation, require a special identification card or training documentation for the dog, or ask that the dog demonstrate its ability to perform the work or task.

Allergies and fear of dogs are not valid reasons for denying access or refusing service to people using service animals. When a person who is allergic to dog dander and a person who uses a service animal must spend time in the same room or facility, for example, in a school classroom or at a homeless shelter, they both should be accommodated by assigning them, if possible, to different locations within the room or different rooms in the facility.

Non-Apparent Disabilities

When you see someone in a wheelchair or travelling with a service dog, you'll know right away that they have a disability. But often disabilities are not obvious. In this section we'll give you some ideas about what people with hidden disabilities may be dealing with, and how you can be supportive and inclusive. If someone you interact with at work or at your place of worship, or while you're travelling, seems to be behaving in a way that's hard to understand, a hidden disability could be what's going on. Instead of being impatient or judgmental, consider compassion along with gentle inquiry.

Following are some examples that might help you become more aware of hidden disabilities that could interfere with a person's ability to communicate, understand,

> *"There is no external sign that I am conversationally handicapped so folks hear some conversational misstep and say "What an arrogant jerk!" I look forward to the day when my handicap will afford me the same respect accorded to a guy in a wheelchair."*
>
> From <u>Look Me In The Eye: My Life with Asperger's</u> by John Elder Robison

or fully participate in what's going on:

- A person might have a less severe form or earlier stage of a disability, such as vision or hearing impairment. If you are having a communication challenge with someone you don't know very well, consider that a physical impairment may be the root cause. Ask the person if there's anything that would make communication easier.

- Someone may have a medical diagnosis or might be undergoing treatment that could have them be especially tired or have difficulty concentrating. Someone undergoing cancer treatment can be in what's described as a "post-chemo fog". Considering alternate reasons might give you that motivation to slow down, and be sensitive and gracious.

- Autism or Asperger's Syndrome may have a person be extremely sensitive to touch and other forms of stimulation including light and noise. If someone you don't know well recoils at a casual touch, this could be the reason.

- People on the Autism spectrum may also be unusually direct in their speech which can be taken as challenging by someone who doesn't understand the dynamics.

- Autoimmune Disorders like Rheumatoid Arthritis may present with chronic pain that can cause irritability. Wouldn't you be irritable if you were in pain all the time?

- MS – Muscular Sclerosis – is another autoimmune disease that can affect the brain and spinal cord, resulting in loss of muscle control, vision, balance, and sensation (such as numbness). You could meet someone who is managing these symptoms, and not have any idea.

- Tourette's Syndrome is characterized by repetitive, involuntary movements. The person may drop things, or have unfamiliar vocalizations. Be gracious and patient. Don't you appreciate being treated that way?

- Learning disabilities like dyslexia or Attention Deficit Disorder can affect a person's ability to read or understand directions.

It's believed that dyslexia accounts for 80 – 90% of learning problems. A common misconception is that people with dyslexia "see letters backwards" but according to the Association for Psychological Science, that's a myth. They explain that dyslexia (meaning "difficulty with words") is a learning disability marked by difficulties in processing written language. People with dyslexia typically experience problems with reading and spelling despite adequate classroom instruction, and may find it challenging to "sound out" and identify printed words.

Well known businessman Charles Schwab, who founded the brokerage firm that bears his name, explains his experience of dyslexia: *"Understanding what letter goes where and why it makes that sound? I don't understand that."*

There are many examples of people with learning disabilities like dyslexia who are known for exceptional creativity and achievement. Richard Branson is the head of 150 or so enterprises that carry the Virgin name, with a personal wealth estimated at nearly $3 billion. It is a success that was never expected for a Dyslexic, nearsighted boy.

Richard reports that he didn't breeze through school. It wasn't just a challenge for him, it was a nightmare. His Dyslexia embarrassed him.

It has long been known that people with Dyslexia are drawn to running their own businesses, where they can get around their weaknesses in reading and writing and play to their strengths. But a study of entrepreneurs in the United States suggests that Dyslexia is much more common among small-business owners than even the experts had thought.

The report, compiled by Julie Logan, a professor of entrepreneurship at the Cass Business School in London, found that more than a third of the entrepreneurs she surveyed - 35 percent - identified themselves as dyslexic. The study also concluded that dyslexics were more likely than non-dyslexics to delegate authority and to excel in oral communication and problem solving and were twice as likely to own two or more businesses.

"We found that dyslexics who succeed had overcome an awful lot in their lives by developing compensatory skills," Logan said during an interview. *"If you tell your friends and acquaintances that you plan to start a business, you'll hear over and over, 'It won't work. It can't be done.' But dyslexics are extraordinarily creative about maneuvering their way around problems."*

> *"I see the end zone of a particular thing quicker. I was moving ahead to conclusion. I go straight from step A to Z, and say: 'This is the outcome. I can see it.'"*
>
> Charles Schwab, Chairman of the discount brokerage firm, on an effect of his dyslexia

But there can also be a dark underside to living with disability that's not apparent.

Lisa Lorden Myers writes about living with Chronic Fatigue Syndrome and Fibromyalgia. In the following excerpt she tells us how access to a parking space for the disabled makes life possible for her...but how her "hidden" disability left her vulnerable to a passerby's criticism: x

> *"It was a clear, sunny day and the weather was glorious. Yet despite the sunshine, I was struggling with excruciating fatigue. I needed to go to the bank and I dragged myself on this one errand, knowing that as soon as I finished, I could return home and lie down. I pulled my car into the parking space closest to the building, between those blue lines that indicate parking for the disabled or handicapped. One of the privileges I have come to count on in coping with my illness is my blue disabled parking permit. When doing an errand or two would be an insurmountable task if not for the ability to park close-by, the blue tag I hang from my rear-view mirror allows me to function in ways I otherwise could not.*
>
> *As I got out of the car, a woman approached me. 'I hope you feel good about parking there,' she said sarcastically. I was caught off guard and responded dumbly, 'What?' and looked at her, not sure if I had heard her correctly. 'I hope you're happy' she said, 'taking a space that's for the handicapped.' My heart was beating furiously. 'I do have a permit,' I stammered. 'Well' she said, disdain all over her face, 'you look like you can walk fine to me—you're about as handicapped as I am!'*

I was stunned. I stood there mute, horrified, but unable to even defend myself. It wasn't until she walked away that the tears began to roll down my face."

Let's not be so quick to judge. We may have no idea what it takes for a person to do a routine errand.

The non-apparent disability may also be associated with brain injury. Brain injuries result from trauma and disease and may present themselves in various ways such as speech impediments (e.g., slurring), mobility or other motor coordination problems, seizure disorders or cognitive difficulties which interfere with understanding and communication. The aftermath of stroke may also present these problems.

Seizure disorders can present a frightening situation. If a person suddenly shows seizure symptoms (such as thrashing, major muscle contractions, loss of consciousness) realize that there is nothing you can do to stop the seizure. You can move the person away from any objects that may harm her and place a pillow or soft object under her head. Otherwise, there's nothing you can do but wait for the seizure to pass. Once it's passed and the person is alert it would be kind to give her some private space to re-orient herself and overcome any embarrassment or confusion. Chances are this is not a first-time event so ask whether or not she needs medical attention. Trust her instincts and your own.

My friend Dan Windheim was involved in a terrible car accident in 1979. He sustained a Traumatic Brain Injury (TBI) which resulted in, among other things, a noticeable speech impediment. Even so, Dan has pursued a successful career as an author and a commentator. Since 2008, Dan has hosted his own radio show called *Dialogues with Dan* on RocklandWorldRadio.com, with guests who speak on many disability-related topics. Dan's unique combination of charm, humor and curiosity has attracted a loyal fan base from around the world.

Nevertheless, Dan has often encountered harsh behavior in his daily life when people become impatient or treat him as though he isn't smart. It's insulting and demoralizing. On a show featuring several guests who sustained TBIs, the general observation made was that many people with these injuries stop going out in public because of the unjust and unflattering assumptions they run into. Because of his speech impediment some people assume he's intellectually limited. Because of his uneven gait, some people assume he's had too much to drink.

Many folks with brain injuries conclude that it's too humiliating, too frustrating and just not worth it to go out.

Among veterans who returned from Iraq and Afghanistan, TBIs are the signature injury. According to the Rand Corporation, nearly 20% of the 1.64 million U.S. service members deployed since 2001 experienced a TBI.[xi]

Returning veterans and others with speech or cognitive impairments are frequently treated impatiently and disrespectfully. This is the disability prejudice that seeps into interactions with hurtful consequences.

If we can all slow down a bit, life can be more gracious for ourselves and everyone around us.

Mental health disorders count as a non-visible disability and, like other disabilities, they occur on a continuum.

Tennis star Rafael Nadal won the 2013 US Open Men's Title and during the match celebrated commentator and former player John McEnroe pointed out that Nadal would not step on the lines on the Court...a classic symptom of OCD (Obsessive Compulsive Disorder). The video showed Nadal clearly stepping over and avoiding the base line.

Similarly, tennis champion Jimmy Connors discussed his OCD symptoms in his 2013 autobiography The Outsider. In televised interviews during the 2013 US Open Connors said his habits of repetitive motion helped him stay balanced.

These superstar athletes don't hide their compulsive behaviors but for many people, an OCD diagnosis remains veiled in secrecy. Dr. Alice Flaherty has undergraduate and medical degrees from Harvard, and a Ph.D. in neuroscience from MIT. Her diagnosis of bipolar disorder is what she credits for her empathy: *"What made me empathic was my depressions......depressions help the doctor aspect of me."*[xii]

In another example of a new openness about mental disorders, New York Presbyterian Hospital featured a television spot about John O'Brien, a Lieutenant Colonel in the U.S. Army who served numerous tours in the Middle East. He returned home with post-traumatic stress disorder (PTSD) and was helped by doctors at New York Presbyterian. Lieutenant Colonel O'Brien showed uncommon courage in stepping forward as a spokesperson for a psychiatric disorder, paving the way for other Veterans to seek the help that can free them from the serious impact of PTSD. [xiii]

Where once there was only shame and stigma about mental disorder we are on a path to greater acceptance. It's the weight of our attitudes and outdated beliefs that's the problem much more than any actual impairment.

Once again, we realize that all of our lives are touched by these issues. The National Institute for Mental Health provides research support to improve outcomes for people with anxiety disorders, eating disorders, schizophrenia and many other conditions.

Nancy Davis wrote <u>Lean on Me: Ten Powerful Steps to Moving Beyond Your Diagnosis and Taking Back Your Life</u> to illustrate an empowered approach to living with a disability that may not be apparent.

> *"I have this little thing hanging over my head. It's telling me to live my life and live every day to its fullest."*
>
> Nancy Davis on her MS disease

According to the Amazon review, the author was a mother of three small children when she was diagnosed with MS at the age of 33. Her neurologist told her to go home and "go to bed... forever." Determined to have an active life, Davis developed a program to live as fully as possible. First she ditched a troubled marriage and surrounded herself only with people who would support her emotionally. She learned as much as she could about MS, working her way through the maze of medical information and misinformation to find which physicians and treatments would be the most help.

More than twenty years after her diagnosis Ms. Davis is still going strong: "I think when people tell you they're taking your life away and you're not going to be able to do anything, you want to get it all in while you still can 'cause you kind of have this fear that tomorrow I'm going to wake up and not be able to do anything. I think it stimulates you more to do those things that you might have not wanted to do."

People Who Look Different

The New York Times published a photograph of a contestant on CBS Television "The Amazing Race," bearing her prosthetic leg for the world to see. The article also quotes Kylee Haddad, whose right leg was amputated below the knee following a car accident, as saying that some people gawk and have told her *"You're upsetting my child.*" But she refuses to hide. "*You either accept me as I am*" she says "*or you don't have to look at me.*"

Just think once again about the monumental change in cultural norms compared with the time when President Franklin Roosevelt's disability was shielded from the public by the press corps.

People who look different may be shorter or taller than the norm, they may have an altered appearance due to due to accident or illness, or they may lack neurological control.

The person may be stared at or even mocked.

But as our culture moves to demand the rights of all people, and as all people claim those rights, we are becoming more accustomed to seeing people who look different.

ABC's "Dancing with The Stars" featured Amy Purdy and her partner Derek Hough. Amy is a double amputee, and her prosthetic limbs carried her with deceptive ease through four weeks of competition according to Sarah Kaufman, The Washington Post's dance critic. The writer comments: "*Peeking out of her adorable gold-fringed cha-cha pants were gleaming metal rods leading to flesh-toned plastic feet, part Terminator, part department store mannequin. Purdy's bionic limbs give her a fascinating fembot-bombshell look.*"

> When the shoe fits, we forget the foot.
>
> Zen saying

Fem-bot is the term dancer Amy Purdy coined in her blog "Through the Eyes of a Fem-Bot".

Writer Kaufman goes on: *"Watching Purdy dance, we forget her disability. It doesn't even seem right to use the word disability. In fact, Purdy is helping to bury the very notion of disability."*

People of short stature are a noteworthy sub-segment of people who look different, because, like deaf people, they have managed to coalesce significant political power. According to the Little People of America online website "such terms as dwarf, little person, and person of short stature are all acceptable but most people would rather be referred to by their name than by a label."

The popular TV series Little People Big World, broadcast on TLC, features the six-member Roloff family. Many of the episodes focus on the parents, Matt and Amy, and one of their sons, Zach, who are diagnosed with dwarfism. This show helps us see that so-called disability is just a small part of the entire dynamic of life for this family. It creates a context for us to see lives in their full complexity.

Sudden or New Onset Disability Versus Disability of Long Duration

Someone confronted with a new disability such as an amputation, or blindness as a complication of diabetes, may react by being scared, embarrassed, angry or feel helpless or depressed. The person may not know what life changes this new diagnosis will bring. By contrast, someone who has had a disability from birth or for a long period has had time to come to terms with the disability, learn how to compensate for it, and know what he or she needs.

In contrast, someone with a temporary disability such as a broken leg or treatable eye infection may not be as emotionally distraught as someone with a permanent disability.

Somebody raised in a pre-ADA compliant world when it was nearly impossible to get around may have learned helpless behavior as a survival mechanism in order to get assistance because of the difficulty in getting around independently. That person may insist on behaving in a childlike way. We suggest that you honor what the person needs first, even though you may violate some principles like speaking directly with the person with the disability and not with a companion accompanying the person.

Let the person with the disability take the lead on how much help he or she wants or doesn't want and the nature of that help.

THE JOURNEY TOWARD INCLUSION

Language

"Jared can be hot-tempered but I'm sure you'll get along with him."

"Maria is an Ivy League graduate."

"JoAnna is disabled."

These labels create expectations. We may avoid controversial topics with the hot-tempered man to stave off his alleged explosive tendencies. We may respect the Ivy League woman before she's earned our respect. And the person who is said to be disabled? This description overrides who the person is and what her capabilities actually are.

JoAnna may be the most skillful accountant in the department or an accomplished scientist but when we describe her as "disabled" it colors every expectation. And if we say "wheelchair bound" we've characterized her as a prisoner of her wheelchair -- a victim -- rather than a person who has made an informed choice about what mobility device to use to get around - motorized or not, collapsible or not, cantilevered wheels or not.

"Wheelchair user" implies choice whereas "wheelchair bound" implies victim. "Wheelchair rider" implies an even greater level of vitality. "Disabled" or "crippled" focuses on the disability whereas the alternative "person with a disability" or "person with Rheumatoid Arthritis," used in an appropriate context, is more accurate, more respectful and more useful.

This distinction – speaking about the "person who" is blind or deaf or has a diagnosis of Rheumatoid Arthritis – is what the "People First" movement is all about[xiv]. It's more than just political correctness. It colors our expectations in ways that are subtle, and not so subtle. And it's important to understand the impact of disrespectful language because it contributes to the backlash against people with disabilities that shows itself in unemployment and underemployment, bullying and isolation of our family and friends who are marginalized.

Think about when you've been spoken to dismissively and the impact it had. Next time you hear someone say, "wheelchair bound" try offering an alternative: *"Oh, you mean he's a wheelchair user?"* We can change language and its impact one brave comment at a time. And if it's done with a smile, even better.

A theme of this book is that many things occur on a continuum. Disabilities occur on a continuum of severity and how much of a problem they are, or aren't.

The evolution of language occurs on a continuum. The way we speak about things changes decade over decade partly as a consequence of evolving cultural norms.

Law

"Press forward at all times, climbing forward toward that
higher ground of the harmonious society that shapes the laws
of man to the laws of God."
Adam Clayton Powell

Law also evolves on a continuum and, as Adam Clayton Powell put it so beautifully, it *"climbs forward toward that higher ground..."*. Hard is it may be to believe, scholars tell us that the ancient world did not even possess the concept of universal human rights[xv]. As we have evolved through thousands of years of human history, our concept of universal human rights -- and our laws -- continue to evolve.

On a windswept corner in the Harlem neighborhood of New York City there stands a strikingly beautiful statue. See it if you can. It's Adam Clayton Powell in the sculpture entitled "Higher Ground".[xvi] At the base of the statue is the inspiring inscription that begins this section. Countless champions of law have devoted their passion and their lives *"toward that higher ground"*.

In the following section we'll give you a brief overview of the legislative breakthroughs that contribute to our climb toward full inclusion.

Protection from Discrimination

The 1990 passage of the ADA (Americans With Disabilities Act) marked the single most critical moment in securing the rights of people with disabilities in the US. The ADA prohibits, under certain circumstances, discrimination based on disability which the legislation defines as physical or mental impairment that substantially limits a major life activity. The ADA applies to employment, public services, accommodations and telecommunications.

This landmark legislation also provides guidelines about making facilities physically accessible by providing accessible parking spaces, routes and aisles, toilets and ramps. And in 2008 important Amendments were passed in order to broaden the definition of disability so that more people could be protected against discrimination.

Access to Housing

In the 1999 Olmstead case[xvii] the Supreme Court held that unjustified segregation of people with disabilities in institutions is discriminatory.

The Supreme Court explained that its holding "reflects two evident judgments." First, "institutional placement of persons who can handle and benefit from community settings perpetuates unwarranted assumptions that persons so isolated are incapable of or unworthy of participating in community life." Second, "confinement in an institution severely diminishes the everyday life activities of individuals, including family relations, social contacts, work options, economic independence, educational advancement, and cultural enrichment."

Notice the beautiful language in the inset where our thoughtful justices talk about the importance of insuring access to everyday life activities including family, work, education and culture. This ruling took a stand against isolation and for inclusion.

Access to Resources

The State Grant for Assistive Technology Program[xviii] supports state efforts to improve the provision of assistive technology to individuals with disabilities of all ages through comprehensive, statewide programs that are consumer responsive. The National Activities program provides information and technical assistance through grants, contracts, or cooperative agreements, on a competitive basis, to individuals, service providers, states, protection and advocacy entities, and others to support and improve the implementation of the AT Act.

Provisions for Education

The Individuals with Disabilities Education Act[xix] is the federal law that supports special education and related service programming for children and youth with disabilities. This federal legislation is designed to ensure that children with disabilities be granted a free appropriate public education in the least restrictive environment. This phrase -- "least restrictive" -- places important emphasis on trying to provide unencumbered access to all the experiences of childhood.

Technology

The progression of law toward "that higher ground" combines with the revolution in technology to create exciting new pathways to full inclusion for people with disabilities.

For children, there are breakthroughs for fuller access to all of the experiences of being a child.

Dr. Cole Galloway is a professor of physical therapy at the University of Delaware. He creates "mobility devices" for crawlers, toddlers and preschoolers who are not able to walk. A child who can't walk will typically be picked up or wheeled in a stroller, severely limiting independence. With the devices built by Dr. Cole and his team, the child can investigate surroundings, explore and learn. These independent activities are crucial to developing social interaction and cognitive progress because they give the child a chance to discover what she likes and what she doesn't like on her own. Her personality can begin to emerge through this exploration in a way that wouldn't be possible if she were always pushed and carried by the adults who care for her.xx

The incredible impact of this cannot be overstated. A child in those early formative months and years of life gains independence and the ability to find ways to work around her physical limitations. As she expands, the world's technology solutions predictably will continue to expand.

Fuller access is being created every day through more technology breakthroughs.

Apple Inc., is the multinational computer company headquartered in Cupertino, California where according to author Alan Brightman *"thousands of young men and women became convinced that 'a personal computer can change your life.'* Brightman served as the Director of Worldwide Disability Solutions. In his beautifully written book DisabilityLand[xxi], Brightman observed that Apple employees devoted endless hours *"working 90 hours a week and loving it"*, where the parking lots, like the bike racks, were always full.

Many of the breakthroughs these enthusiasts developed open worlds of opportunity for children and adults with disabilities. For example, the Apple iPhone offers a free application called ArtikPix, a flashcard activity app that allows students to practice speech. iPhone also offers ADHD Angel to help students understand their condition and monitor and manage their feelings. The app is designed to set up reminders for medications, to create files to share with clinicians, to provide a template for monitoring mood and to allow syncing with a parent or caregiver's computer or smartphone.

Apple has spent years continuing to develop "The Alex Voice", a text-to-speech system that now analyzes a paragraph at a time to decipher the context of words more accurately so that its speech has a much more natural quality sound, including breaths of the speaker.

This is an invaluable technology resource for anyone who has difficulty reading, for any reason. You can easily find tutorials on-line, and if you experiment, you will be amazed at how written words will be read to you from your device.

My friend and colleague Suzanne Robitaille authored The Illustrated Guide to Assistive Technology and Devices: Tools and Gadgets for Living Independently[xxii]. Suzanne is an accomplished journalist who has written for The Wall Street Journal and other prestigious publications. In her journey growing up profoundly deaf, she learned firsthand how people with disabilities benefit from technology both professionally and socially.

If you, or anyone you know, might benefit from assistive technology, do consider getting this comprehensive book. It has sections on technologies for people with visual, hearing, physical, cognitive disabilities and more. It even has a section on how to pay for assistive technology. Suzanne keeps abreast of new "tools and gadgets" on her vibrant website AbledBody.com subtitled "where can-do is done different". If you visit you'll get the idea that the people who participate are truly "can-do" people.

Medicine and Medical Devices

When my mother had her leg amputated in the late 1980's due to vascular complications from Rheumatoid Arthritis, she struggled to be able to walk with the prosthetic devices of the day. Today these devices make walking much easier.

In 2013 the New York Times published "War and Sports Shape Better Artificial Limbs"[xxiii], an article that highlighted the experience of John Kremer, a Navy explosives expert who lost both his legs in Afghanistan in 2010.

According to the article, prosthetic technology has advanced significantly, with computerized knees and ankles that adjust to terrain and activity enabling Mr. Kremer to run, swim and bike almost daily and to compete in swimming, shooting, seated volleyball and wheelchair basketball.

Hugh Herr, head of the MIT Media Lab's Biomechatronics research group, spoke at TED 2014 about his group's work in creating bionic prosthetic limbs, and their goal to eliminate human disability through technology.

> "I didn't view my body as broken. I reasoned that a human being can never be broken."
> Hugh Herr on the amputation of his legs

Herr explained: *"Bionics explores the interplay between biology and design. My legs are bionic. Electromechanics are beginning to bridge the gap between disability and ability, between human limitation and human potential. Bionics has defined my physicality. In 1982 both of my legs were amputated due to tissue damage resulting from frostbite that occurred during a mountain climbing accident. During that time I didn't view my body as broken. I reasoned that a human being can never be broken. Technology is inadequate. This simple but powerful idea was a call to arms to advance technology to eliminate my own disability and ultimately the disability of others."*

Advances in medicine have also changed the way people live with diseases like cancer, heart disease and aids. The natural occurrence of some cancers, like ovarian, is of recurrence and remission. This repeating cycle can translate into survival over many years during which the cancer is managed as a chronic illness.[xxiv]

There are many other chronic conditions that people manage, for example more than one million people in the US are living with HIV Infection[xxv].

When we are at work, or at church or mosque, or when we're travelling - at any time we may be with someone who is benefiting from the medical advances that prolong life. And that person may also be dealing with consequences of the treatment.

Unless we have reason to know the person's medical circumstances, we may only see fatigue, distractedness, or irritability. As we continue on our journey toward full inclusion let's open our hearts to compassion for another's circumstances. It's how we move *"toward that higher ground of a more harmonious society."*

EMPLOYMENT: ISSUES AND OPPORTUNITIES

"When you are born, your work is placed in your heart."

Kahlil Gibran

When Americans meet, our customary first question to each other is *"What do you do?"* It's our identity. Our employment is generally how we put a roof over our heads and how we feed ourselves. It's pivotal to survival. And yet too many people are denied employment due to myths and misconceptions about disability.

The Magnitude of Unemployment

The statistics that measure unemployment among people with disabilities have remained largely unchanged over decades despite legal, technical and medical advances.

According to the Bureau of Labor Statistics, only 21% of people with a disability over age 16 are in the labor force. That compares with 70% of people without a disability. [xxvi]

Many people with disability who are unemployed are physically, mentally and functionally capable of participating in the workforce.

Disability prejudice is at least one important factor blocking full access to paid employment.

Imagine you stop by your local Wal-Mart and the greeter is a wheelchair user. Imagine your bank teller hands you your bills with her prosthetic arm. Imagine the candidate whose resume looks really good reveals that he's diabetic and injects with insulin.

Do you notice your moment's hesitation? Your eyes widen, just for a split second?

That is disability prejudice, at its most visceral.

Leaders in the human resource field know that disability prejudice – like all prejudice – is a problem in the workplace, giving weight to myths and misconceptions and disrupting harmony.

The leaders at the Society for Human Resource Management (SHRM) published the results of an illustrative study in HR Magazine. [xxvii] The study found that 50% of the HR professionals polled said people with disabilities could not adequately perform required work duties. Topping the reasons for these conclusions: 25% cited lack of knowledge about the disabled as the primary deterrent, another 24% mentioned concern about cost of workplace adjustments and accommodations, and 15% admitted a lack of understanding about accommodations.[xxviii]

Imagine, half of our human resource managers admitted their bias, that a person with a disability couldn't perform adequately knowing nothing else and based solely on that charged word.

Most Workplace Accommodation is Neither Difficult nor Expensive

A reasonable accommodation is a modification or adjustment to a job, the work environment, or the way things usually are done that enables a qualified individual with a disability to enjoy an equal employment opportunity. Examples of reasonable accommodations include:

- making existing facilities accessible
- job restructuring
- part-time or modified work schedules
- acquiring or modifying equipment
- changing tests, training materials, or policies
- providing qualified readers or interpreters
- reassignment to a more suitable position[xxix]

According to the US Department of Labor Office of Disability Employment Policy[xxx], an accommodation can be simple, such as putting blocks under a table's legs so that a person who uses a wheelchair can roll up to it. It might involve technology, such as providing access to a screen reader that identifies and interprets what's being displayed on the computer screen. This makes documents available to the person who is visually impaired or who has difficulty reading for other reasons. The accommodation may be procedural, such as altering a work schedule or job assignment.

When we think about accommodations, the focus should be on the essential job task, not the person's disability. Consider a receptionist who cannot answer the phone because he or she can't grasp the receiver. A handle could be attached to the receiver to enable him or her to balance it on the hand. Or, the receptionist could use a headset, eliminating the need for grasping altogether.

The reason the person can't grasp the material is immaterial. With a simple accommodation, the employee can answer the phone.

> **Don't let your eyes do the judging.**
>
> One day a young woman walked into an interview for a job as a data entry operator and she had no arms. The interviewer wasn't fazed and knew how to deal with the situation. *'You understand that you have to data enter at 85 words per minute. I notice you have no arms, can you tell me how you can manage that requirement?'* 'Yes, I have a very long cord for my keyboard and I type 95 words a minute with my toes.'

Devising accommodations can uncover strategies that help others, regardless of whether they have disabilities.

For example, headsets may help other receptionists perform their duties with less neck strain.

Magnifying glasses at work stations help people with visual disabilities read documents and may reduce eye strain for others.

Think of curb cuts. These were designed to enable people who use wheelchairs to get on and off sidewalks but they routinely benefit people pushing strollers or carts.

Ensuring that the needs of workers with disabilities are met can benefit the entire workforce.

The Job Accommodation Network (JAN) is a free and confidential service from the U.S. Department of Labor's Office of Disability Employment Policy that provides individualized accommodation solutions. They report that two-thirds of accommodations cost less than $500, with nearly a quarter costing nothing at all.

The Particular Stigma of Depression and Related Mood Disorders: Strategies for Inclusion

About 12% of workers have been diagnosed with depression at some point. These workers miss an estimated 68 million additional days of work each year than their counterparts who have not been depressed -- resulting in an estimated cost of more than $23 billion in lost productivity annually to U.S. employers.[xxxi]

And most people, through shame and the reaction to stigma, do not seek help. Only 29% of people with depression reported contacting a mental health professional in the past year[xxxii]

Theresa, a senior manager at a professional services firm, is known for her charm, her wit and her broad base of clinical and business skills. But whenever her responsibilities expand she begins to ramp up in excitement and energy that soon escalates into a state that her doctor has diagnosed as mania, a mood disorder characterized by wide mood swings – from depression to mania -- accompanied by an alarming sleeplessness. She knows that the sleepless nights result in impaired judgment the following day so she agreed to begin a course of drug therapy even though she had mixed feelings about doing so: *"Now I have that label. Am I crazy? What do I tell people?"*

Often people like Theresa don't know where to go for help on how to navigate their illness while remaining productively employed.

Many workplaces offer Employee Assistance Programs (EAPs) designed to help businesses and organizations address productivity issues by helping employees identify, and then resolve, personal concerns that affect job performance. EAPs have been shown to contribute to:

- decreased absenteeism
- reduced accidents and fewer workers compensation claims
- greater employee retention
- fewer labor disputes and
- significantly reduced medical costs arising from early identification and treatment of individual mental health and substance abuse issues.

According to the Department of Labor, EAPs are unique in that they provide services to individual employees and family members and to the employer/work organization as a whole.

Leadership in Inclusion

While there's no doubt that unemployment among people with disability is a serious barrier to full inclusion, there are bright lights on the horizon.

Major companies have committed to diversity and inclusion because it's the right thing to do. A person's disability is peripheral to their skills and abilities. In an inclusive corporate culture hiring managers are urged to look past the disability to see the capability and invest in human potential.

Forbes Insights[xxxiii] surveyed 321 executives with direct responsibility or oversight for their companies' diversity and inclusion programs. All respondents worked for large global enterprises with annual revenues of more than US$500 million. More than 40% worked for companies with annual revenues of US$5 billion or more.

According to the study, diversity is a key driver of innovation and is a critical component of being successful on a global scale. Senior executives are recognizing that a diverse set of experiences, perspectives, and backgrounds is crucial to innovation and the development of new ideas. When asked about the relationship between diversity and innovation, a majority of respondents agreed that diversity is crucial to encouraging different perspectives and ideas that foster innovation.

America's largest drug store chain, Walgreens, is a great example of a progressive company that's made concrete and measureable progress. Under the leadership of Senior Vice President Randy Lewis, in 2007 Walgreen's opened the first facility of its kind to employ a significant number of people with disabilities.

As is the case with many disability champions, Lewis has direct experience with the challenges faced by people with disability. Being father of a severely autistic son, now in his twenties, he always had a longing to work out how business could make better use of people with disabilities. *"It stems from me knowing what my son would be facing and all the parents like me who wish they could live one day longer than their child"* he says. *"The worry is how are they going to take care of themselves?"*

Walgreens had previously employed people with disability to do *"ancillary rather than mission-critical work"*, working for cleaning contractors for example, but Lewis wanted to do something more. *"We wanted an opportunity to bring people in as our employees"* he recalls.

Retail is a notoriously competitive environment, with razor thin margins. When Lewis proposed his vision for a new distribution center with his board, he knew saying he planned to invest significantly would not go down well with the shareholders.

"We never lost sight of the fact that we are a business, not a charity. This had to make business sense. We had to hold everyone to the same standards and have a completely inclusive environment. When I presented it to the board I said this was going to be the most

expensive building we had ever built, which they didn't like, but I said it was also going to have the best ROI (return on investment), be the most efficient and be built in such a way that one-third of the workforce would be disabled."[xxxiv]

Turned out that more than 40% of the distribution center's workforce has a physical or cognitive impairment such as autism or a developmental disability. The total investment for this center was more than $175 million.[xxxv]

New Walgreens centers have since opened with the same design and workforce inclusion elements in mind. Employees with disabilities have been trained to work side-by-side with other team members - with the same productivity goals, earning the same pay. An on-site training facility helps those with special needs become prepared for employment so everyone can work productively and effectively.

In Walgreen's distribution centers today an average 35% of the workforce comprises people with disabilities and it has set targets to make sure one in every 10 in-store hires has a disability.

Randy Lewis is now retired, but the culture of Walgreen's bears the imprint of his pioneering vision. And the business case for an inclusive workplace remains strong according to Steve Pemberton, Chief Diversity Officer, who recognizes that misconceptions still exist among executives at other companies: *"We need to sail right at what the concerns are. Companies expect to see a spike in worker compensation and safety problems but that is not grounded in any real empirical experience with companies like Walgreens who have been successful."*

Professional Safety magazine is published by The Journal of the American Society of Safety Engineers. Their report about the 10,000 employees at Walgreens Supply Chain and Logistics Division debunks the myth that employees with disability are more expensive to employ and less safe than the general workforce.[xxxvi] They also report:

- Better retention for workers with disability
- Comparable productivity between workers with and without disability

This journal highlights a particularly interesting finding about fork lift drivers who are deaf or hearing impaired. Walgreens' lift truck fleet consists of approximately 1500 vehicles and 3400 certified drivers. A significant minority of drivers are deaf or hearing impaired and the findings show that the team members with disabilities had 34% fewer incident/accident events than the remaining population. The management team hypothesized that deaf drivers are not distracted by additional noise and therefore can concentrate more fully on the task at hand, which leads to improved safety performance.

The journal also reports that employees with disclosed disabilities incur:

> *It's better for everybody when it's better for everybody.*
> Eleanor Roosevelt

- Costs for medical treatment that are 67% less than the contrasting population
- Costs for indemnity/time off that are 73% less than the contrasting population and
- Expense costs that are 77% less than the contrasting population

A large distribution operation like Walgreens gives us the opportunity to study the good business outcomes that employees with disability create – better retention, fewer safety issues and comparable productivity rates, fewer expenses for medical treatment and time off.

Walgreens also puts resources in place at both the division and the building level including a manager responsible for meeting hiring and retention goals, a human resource professional who ensures compliance and maintains records, a safety process manager responsible for safety training and even external job coaches from outside agencies who provide initial candidate screening and training services.

In the wider world of jobs, employees with disability are distributed throughout our workplaces where they don't exist in sufficient numbers to generate this type of measurement – or such extensive support - but they do provide illustrative evidence of the profound benefit of fostering inclusiveness.

- The established professional with the late onset of a disability re-enters the workplace. He is experienced and proficient in the job-at-hand. To ensure a successful back to work transition, all that might be needed is to acculturate his immediate co-workers to the colleague's new circumstance through a brief training session where candid questions are welcomed to diffuse any tension or awkwardness.
- A new graduate with disability is seeking an entry level position in law, finance, or another field with good growth potential. This candidate brings the energy and enthusiasm of the new graduate combined with the tenacity and character often associated with achieving a degree in the presence of the barriers that disability may present.
- A candidate with an intellectual disability may be well into adulthood before landing that first paid job. Andy Traub, as director of recruitment at AMC Theatres, revamped the hiring process and started walking applicants through the building to show them what their responsibilities might be. By gauging the candidates' reaction to various tasks, AMC matches the employee to the job that best suits them.[xxxvii]

Government Takes the Lead

In America, progress in human rights has often been facilitated by government intervention. In that tradition we are now seeing leadership in opening employment opportunities at both the state and federal levels.

For many years people with intellectual disabilities have been employed at so-called "sheltered workshops", working at repetitive jobs for little pay and in isolation. A federal investigation turned a Rhode Island workshop upside down after abuses were revealed, including withholding earned pay from workers with disability.

Working with the Department of Justice's civil rights division, the State of Rhode Island agreed to help the workshop's clients find employment and day services in the community – an agreement followed up by a landmark consent decree that requires similar integrated opportunities for 2,000 other clients around the state, completely transforming Rhode Island's sheltered workshop system.

The decree has put the 49 other states on notice that in the eyes of the federal government, sheltered workshops can no longer be default employment services for people with disabilities, most of whom can, with support, thrive in the workplace.[xxxviii]

At the Federal level, significant change is underway with the new Section 503 regulations which compel businesses to significantly increase the number of people with disabilities that they employ.[xxxix]

The rule requires most federal contractors to ensure that people with disabilities account for at least 7 percent of workers within each job group in their workforce.

While officials at the U.S. Department of Labor say they are not establishing a firm hiring quota for contractors, they do expect that businesses servicing the government will work toward achieving the target. Contractors that fail to meet the goal and do not show sufficient effort toward reaching the 7 percent threshold could lose their contracts under the new rule.

Disability advocates say the added pressure on federal contractors will have a significant impact on opportunities for candidates with disability.

"Federal contractors represent 22 percent of the American workforce and an aspirational 7 percent hiring goal means the rule will create real jobs, at all levels of seniority, for Americans with disabilities," said Mark Perriello, president and CEO of the American Association of People with Disabilities.

Perriello said he expects that the government's new requirement for contractors will ultimately have a ripple effect throughout the economy, with the potential to transform employment opportunities for people with disabilities.

Under the rule, businesses with at least 50 employees and $50,000 in federal contracts must take specific steps surrounding recruitment, training, record keeping and policy dissemination, all designed to up employment of those with disabilities. Similar steps are already required to promote inclusion of women and minorities in the workplace.

The changes could mean up to 585,000 jobs for people with disabilities within the first year alone, the Labor Department said when the rule was finalized.[xl]

In addition to government interventions, associations can also make a difference in providing important assistance.

The US Business Leadership Network® (USBLN®) is a national non-profit that helps business drive performance by leveraging disability inclusion in the workplace, supply chain, and marketplace.

The USBLN® serves as the collective voice of nearly 50 Business Leadership Network affiliates across the United States, representing over 5,000 businesses.

Additionally, the USBLN® Disability Supplier Diversity Program® (DSDP) is the nation's leading third-party certification program for disability-owned businesses, including businesses owned by service-disabled veterans.

Disability Can Uncover Assets and Improve Harmony

Walgreens and other progressive corporations have taken the lead in providing empirical evidence about the absence of excessive risk that some employers have feared.

But less risk is just part of the picture. Sometimes people who have overcome significant barriers develop character traits that are apparent to the people around them. At a workshop[xli] among people who serve college students with disabilities, participants generated a list of attributes that they notice among these students, including an exceptional level of:

- Passion
- Energy
- Tenacity
- Perseverance
- Empathy
- Flexibility
- Patience
- Strategic thinking
- Problem solving
- Being collaborative

Richard Paszkiet, one of the collaborators on this book, pointed out that when he commutes to his job in Chicago, he notices the softening of attitudes in fellow passengers when a wheelchair user is boarding: *"I ride the L every morning. Everyone is very understanding."* And in the supermarket, that routinely hires people with development disabilities to bag groceries, there's a palpable sense of appreciation that diversity is part of the store's hiring culture.

John D. Kemp, Esq. is President & CEO of The Viscardi Center, a non-profit organization that provides a life span of services that educate, employ and empower people with disabilities. As a person with a disability who uses four prostheses, that is, prosthetic devices for arms and for legs, he inspires others to achieve the impossible through knowledge, experience, vision, personality, and persistence.

Anyone who meets John can sense that he is a happy man. He's happily married. He travels the world. He is legendary for his many achievements. He received the Henry B. Betts Award, America's most prestigious award within the national disability community which honors an individual whose work and scope of influence have significantly improved the quality of life for people with disabilities.

He has received top awards from the US Departments of Labor and Health and Human Services.

Mr. Kemp was a partner in the DC's Powers, Pyles, Sutter & Verville, P.C. Law Firm. He has served as General Counsel and Vice President - Development for the National Easter Seal Society and managed law and consulting firms that advised companies on state and federal civil rights, employment and education laws and policies regarding persons with disabilities.

But even more legendary is his incredible charm and capacity to make anyone feel comfortable.

John knows firsthand the assets that disability can uncover. As he puts it: *"Because of my disability, I can accept a lot. We have to lift ourselves up just to be equal. People always see me as different. 'What happened to you?' I am constantly being asked."*

Staff, students, and parents of students served by the Viscardi Center regard John Kemp as a model of leadership and achievement. He provides others with a sense of hope for themselves, that they too can achieve a full and happy life.

> *All a disability means is that you may have to work harder to accomplish what you want to get done.* – Recent Graduate Richard

Richard is just one example.[xlii] Since he was a young boy, Richard has been outgoing, goal oriented and a natural leader. A student at the Henry Viscardi School at The Viscardi Center for the past 12 years, Richard recently graduated at the top of his class and has set his sights on becoming a civil law attorney so he can help others with disabilities.

In addition to being an excellent role model for the elementary and high school students at Henry Viscardi School, Richard has been mentoring young, first-time campers at the Southampton Fresh Air Home, a summer camp for physically challenged children ages 7 to 18, for the past several years.

One of three triplet boys, with an older brother too, Richard will be dorming at Adelphi and looks forward to living on his own. *"It's a big step but I am looking to become more independent,"* he explained along with how he felt the teachers and staff at Henry Viscardi School had prepared him for this new experience, which included overnights at The Viscardi Center's Independent Living House where he learned everyday life skills like planning meals, cooking and cleaning.

He also plans to actively participate in college campus activities and clubs, including the student government where he thinks he can lend a voice to issues facing fellow classmates with disabilities.

Richard credits Henry Viscardi School with encouraging him to set the bar high and dreaming big. His words of wisdom for children and adults with disabilities, *"Even though you have a disability it doesn't mean you should give up… all a disability means is that you may have to work harder to accomplish what you want to get done. It may be difficult sometimes, but you never should give up."*

The Future: Students in Transition

Suzanne Mackey is one of those Moms who presents like a lion when she's fighting for her children. Her daughter Carrie was born in 1983 with a significant hearing impairment and her Mom fought tooth and nail for Carrie to have every bit of assistance possible from her Clarkstown, New York school system. Ten years later son Kyle came along, born with a significant cleft palate that compromised his ability to speak. Once again, Mom Suzanne devoted every ounce of her energy to advocacy for Kyle.

Both Carrie and Kyle graduated from college and both have created successful careers for themselves.

This Mom is in a unique position to see how support for students with disabilities changed in just ten short years. She says: *"It's amazing the difference in what was available to Kyle, just ten years later. And I hope that we see more and more advancement because it's so worth it. Kyle and Carrie will both repay what's been invested in them many times over as productive workers and taxpayers."*

Today, virtually every campus in the US has a Disability Services Office staffed with knowledgeable people who can help students get the most from their education by providing advice, support and accommodation.

But too often students flounder when they endeavor to go into the workplace because the support isn't there to the same extent. The student is much more on his own.

John Little is a renowned expert in workforce development and founder of the Successful Resumes Consultancy with offices on four continents[xliii]. John, a wheelchair user himself, has mentored countless graduates with disability as they navigate through the job search and interview process. Candidates who come to John and the experts in his group are advised and guided through the process with guidelines including:

- The importance of focusing on personal assets and attributes. Employers want to know not only what the candidate can do but even more importantly the personal attributes and characteristics like tenacity and perseverance – attributes that have often been well developed in the candidate with disability.

- Taking great care in the decision about whether to disclose the disability. If a candidate has a well-controlled medical or mental health condition, he may not need any accommodation and he may not need to disclose his disability at all if he or she is worried about being stigmatized as a result.

  On the other hand, a person with an obvious disability (for example, being of short stature, being blind or a wheelchair user) might best reveal the disability before the interview so the hiring manager isn't caught unawares. But these decisions need to be carefully considered in the context of the employing organization. Federal contractors who seek to meet new hiring targets will ask candidates whether they do or do not have a disability without requesting specifics in order to achieve the targeted levels of disability employment.

- Social media like LinkedIn (www.linkedin.com) provide critical advantages to all candidates but many people undervalue the importance and/or don't know how to use these tools. All candidates – and especially candidates with disability – need to step up their approach to the job search in these competitive times.

LinkedIn, in particular, provides people with disability access to many different disability-centric groups populated by experts and "ordinary people" who have diverse experiences and can aid the candidate's judgment on how to approach issues like disclosure.

Ashley Jones Lawrence is a not for profit executive who has a significant visual impairment. When she relocated to a different city with her husband, she needed to make new connections: *LinkedIn made all the difference for me in being able to find those networking contacts that helped me navigate in new surroundings.*"

Suzanne Colbert has been a lifelong advocate for people with disabilities and thought leader creating breakthrough programs. Her organization, The Australian Network on Disability[xliv], serves multinational corporations like IBM, McDonald's and others to advance the inclusion of people with disability in all aspects of business. Their unique "Stepping Into…" program provides paid internships in law, human resources, accounting and other disciplines designed specifically for university students with disability.

During the past ten years the program has provided breakthrough experiences for hundreds of graduates and has continued to develop and refine supporting materials that are made available to the growing segment of corporate workforce professionals who want to bring students with disability on board in an orderly and well supported way.

Just one of many testimonials shown below illustrate the profound benefits that students with disability bring to their new workplace:

> *"Our candidate brought a really fresh way of thinking to the firm... he looked at problems from new angles and was very solution focused. He had an excellent level of legal knowledge and understanding, and was a very engaging personality to have in the team... We would like to offer him an ongoing role in the firm."* Sparke Helmore Lawyers

All of us who support creating a more inclusive world may find specific and tangible ways to contribute to employment opportunities for people with disability: by reframing prejudicial comments whenever we hear them (*"Wheelchair-bound? Don't you mean wheelchair-user?"*) and by taking the initiative to propose that something else is possible for the unduly worried employer or the floundering candidate.

CREATING A WELCOMING ENVIRONMENT

"The world is so empty if one thinks only of mountains, rivers & cities; but to know someone who thinks & feels with us, & who....is close to us in spirit, this makes the earth for us an inhabited garden."

Goethe

Big Business

The community of people with disability has caught the eye of the corporate world, and of the investment world.

The population of people with disability is the fastest growing minority in the world. Globally, it's about 1.3 billion people, a market roughly the size of China. Add friends and family to the mix and the number doubles to more than half the world's population, according to Rich Donovan a globally recognized subject matter expert on the convergence of disability and corporate profitability.

Donovan, who has cerebral palsy, is CEO of the Return on Disability Group which has partnered with Barclays to create a fund designed to provide investors with exposure to US-based companies that have acted to attract and serve people with disabilities – and their friends and family – as customers and employees. [xlv]

As we saw in the previous chapter, large and multinational organizations like Walgreen's have committed to improving the employment picture for people with disability and many have adopted disability-friendly policies throughout their organizations.

Many large and multinational businesses have resources in place for customers with disability because, according to the Society for Human Resource Management (SHRM), customers with disability represent $220 Billion in discretionary spending power in the US alone.[xlvi]

In the hospitality sector, the Wyndham Hotel Group provides special training for employees to be courteous, comfortable and knowledgeable working with travelers with disability. According to Roy Flora, Group President[xlvii], *"You can't just rely on a manual or a checklist. It's not just about compliance with the law; it's about building our business."* Flora said that means tapping into the millions of travelers with disabilities with billions of their dollars in discretionary income. The Group's Microtel brand provides detailed information for travelers with disabilities, describing room layout and accessibility features including items such as levered door handles which are easier to grasp for people with arthritis or other difficulty opening a conventional doorknob. And like many accessible design features that benefit the public at large, those levered door handles are a boon the general population – for example, to anyone with an armload of packages.

As another example, the hotel group caters to little people and others of short stature by providing a "short stature accessibility kit" complete with step stool, reach grabber and closet rod adapter.

The megabrand Disney makes sure its theme parks are accessible to people with a wide range of abilities. Some rides are designed so wheelchair users can wheel themselves on board, while other rides enable guests to transfer from a chair or scooter to the ride. However, to make sure that they are comfortable doing so, Disney provides a  behind the scenes "practice session" so guests can try transferring to the type of seat used on a particular ride before trying the real thing.

To make sure guests with hearing impairments can enjoy its parks fully, Disney provides scheduled performances with theatrically trained sign language interpreters as well as assistive listening and video captioning services. Guests with visual impairment have access to Braille maps and guidebooks as well as recorded audio descriptions of rides and services.

According to Greg Hale, vice president and chief safety officer of worldwide safety and accessibility for Walt Disney Parks and Resorts, *"We've received a lot of awards but that's not why we did it. We don't want anyone in the family to be left out."*[xlviii]

Another example of corporate commitment to inclusion comes from McDonald's, the fast food giant. They reaped unexpected benefits from a marketing effort

> With Applebee's "See You Tomorrow" ad campaign, they couldn't care less if you can see them back. The casual dining restaurant offers large print and Braille menus as part of their commitment to ensure an inclusive dining experience.

according to Kevin Bradley, the company's director of diversity and inclusion: *"When we featured the first parathlete on one of our bags, consumers started calling our 800 number to say 'That was so cool, thank you so much!'. Every person with a disability has a friend, a loved one, a counselor, so if they are thinking positively about your company because of an ad, that's probably affecting 5 or 10 other folks."*[xlix]

In addition to supporting customers with disability, large companies recognize the need to support employees from various diversity segments and an important way to do that is through affinity groups – also known as employee resource groups or networks. Affinity groups have been formed for ethnic segments (African American, Hispanic), for lifecycle segments (parents of young children), Veterans and others. These groups represent the interests of the members and promote outreach throughout the organization's culture.

The Disability Forum at Booz Allen Hamilton annually hosts a guest speaker program for the July 26th ADA Anniversary. Their

Disability Forum has partnered with other groups where their interests intersect: with the Parents Forum on a program about special education resources and with the Armed Services Forum on an outreach effort to veterans with disabilities. According to author Dr. Robert S. Rudney[l], the idea is to embed disability events and activities in the larger universe of corporate diversity programs.

Affinity groups also benefit companies by providing insight on broadening the appeal of their products and services. Best Buy's affinity group was instrumental in convincing the company to provide an in-store closed-captioning option for its home theater promotions to appeal to prospective customers with hearing impairments. And the auto industry is also on board as Ford Employees Dealing with Disability (FEDA) reviews new cars for accessibility.[li]

Small Business

Smaller businesses are also learning to adapt to the needs and wants of the disability market. Businesses with fewer than 20 workers account for 90% of employer firms in the US according to U.S. Census Bureau data[lii] so it's imperative that good resources are available to owners and managers of small firms.

The US Small Business Administration and the Department of Justice have collaborated to produce a user-friendly publication entitled the "ADA Guide for Small Business".[liii] The authors recognize that businesses have many pressures on limited resources and so they have gone to great lengths to provide "readily accessible" solutions that make businesses more welcoming to people with mobility, vision, hearing and other disabling conditions. The guideline may be as simple as training staff to be welcoming by offering to reach things on a high shelf for someone who can't easily reach it or providing pricing or other information using paper and pencil for the deaf customer. Workable solutions do not need to be burdensome.

Mark Park, Founder of technology innovator Jibbio, recently launched JACK™, a comprehensive resource that provides easy, affordable web-based tools for business to be disability-friendly. According to Park, *"This gives small business access to a customer base which is often overlooked. The response has been overwhelmingly positive, as business owners and managers gain the know-how to be inclusive and welcoming to all customers."*

A disability friendly business strives to be inclusive in five general areas:

- <u>Customer service</u> addresses business practices and staff training
- <u>Information[liv] and communications</u> addresses the removal of barriers in access to information being provided in person, through print material, websites or other means.

- The "built environment" refers to access into and within buildings and outdoor spaces and includes things like counter height, aisle and door width, parking and signs.

- Employment accessibility covers recruitment, hiring, and retention policies and practices.

- Transportation inclusiveness may mean awareness about whether a retail location can be accessed through disability-friendly public transportation or whether a hotel's airport shuttle can accommodate a wheelchair user.

Creating a Welcoming Environment At Home

Imagine you're having a Super Bowl party and your college age son invites his roommate. And you know that his roommate has a disability.

What shall you do?

The first thing to do is to ask your son whether his friend needs any accommodation or whether there's anything in particular you should know.

If he's a wheelchair user he may simply need a clear pathway into the family room through the garage as well as unobstructed access to the bathroom -- which may require some measuring to be sure the chair will fit through the door.

If your son's roommate has food allergies, get the details. If your college age men are like the ones in our family, they may not be quite so careful to give you the specifics so you may want to check with the guest directly.

Your son's roommate may have Asperger's Syndrome (a so-called "Autism spectrum disorder") but knowing the diagnosis doesn't tell you much about the young man. He may have some unusual ways of relating to others or he may exhibit some repetitive movements. He and your son have a relationship, though, so together they'll undoubtedly enjoy a wonderful party at your home. There may be nothing in particular to do, or not do, other than to be welcoming and gracious hosts.

You may want to invite an older neighbor to your party. Age-related hearing loss may be an issue for you to be aware of.

Approximately one third of Americans between ages 65 and 74 and nearly half of those over age 75 have hearing loss. Unfortunately, only 20% of people who might benefit from treatment actually seek help. Most tend to delay treatment until they cannot communicate even in the best of listening situations. On average, hearing aid users wait over 10 years after their initial diagnosis to be fit with their first set of hearing aids.[lv]

Be aware that competing noises from the TV, the adult guests and the kids can make it very difficult for someone with a hearing impairment to follow any of the action. See if, together, you can find a space in the house that insulates him a bit, where he can comfortably watch the game.

A Welcoming Environment at Religious Services and Other Community Events

Our churches, synagogues and mosques are dedicated to creating safe and welcoming space for worshipers. Yet leaders are mindful that their services may not be accessible to all people. Pastor Martha Epstein of Gardnertown United Methodist church expressed concern that the building – first constructed more than 150 years ago – doesn't offer congregants the access of newer churches.

Many leaders worry that the ADA is rigid and requires lots of money to make existing facilities accessible. But the fact is that the ADA is based on common sense. It recognizes that altering existing structures is more costly than making new construction accessible. The law only requires that public accommodations remove architectural barriers in existing facilities when it is "readily achievable", i.e., it can be done "without much difficulty or expense." Inexpensive, easy steps to take include:

- ramping one step;
- installing a bathroom grab bar;
- lowering a paper towel dispenser;
- rearranging furniture to widen pathways;
- installing offset hinges to widen a doorway;
- or painting new lines to create an accessible parking space.[lvi]

In a worship community the most important thing may simply be for congregants to watch out for each other. Offer a ride to a fragile neighbor when weather is bad. Read the newsletter to someone who has difficulty seeing. Check in with the skier who is managing with a broken leg.

Creating a welcoming environment is a state of our mind as much as it's a state of our built environment.

Bonnie Wind is the Director of Adult Services at the JCC – Jewish Community Center – in a northern suburb of New York City. This vibrant organization serves a culturally-diverse assortment of 2700 members with programs for adults and children in sports, recreation, cultural activities and more. According to Wind, Seniors are an especially important part of the organization representing nearly 1000 of its members and making it the third largest Senior center in New York State. *"This age group is among the most vibrant we serve in how they participate in everything we have to offer. They represent our most important pool of volunteers, helping with our preschool and adolescent activities because they've got free time and the inclination to share. Their contributions to our fundraising are enormous."*

Ms. Wind notes that Seniors move in and out of disabling conditions: *"They have new knees. They have new hips. They have new breasts. We have a woman in her mid-eighties and she had a mastectomy and we think 'Why does she need new breasts?' She didn't want to wear a bra with pads, she wants breasts."*

Wind acknowledges that many of the older members have diminished hearing or vision, and some use walkers, some have chronic conditions that require intervention. But she is adamant: *"These are not disabled people."*

Alma Carroll runs the Senior Knitting Group program whose members create beautiful handmade scarves and other wearable items that are sold to fund other programs. Alma, who is 87 at this writing, says: *"It's a great cooperative. It's social. And it's purposeful."* And it benefits her hands, which have been affected by arthritis: *"The doctors tell you, knitting is the best thing you can do."*

Cecile Rojer Jeruchim is a part time employee in her 80s who runs a popular aerobics class called "Boomers in Motion". Cecile experienced a disabling incident: *"I fell on New Year's Day 2012 and I got my broken ankle. I didn't think of it as a disability, I'm thinking it's going to heal. I was out January, February March then I broke my foot and was out another three months."*

Cecile then resumed her teaching duties leading a class for men and women ranging in age through their 90s. *"I choreographed the course myself because I'm a Senior and I know what's good."* Cecile, a Holocaust survivor, explained that she was always a good dancer, *"even in the convent where I was hidden"* after the Nazis took her parents away.

These days, Cecile bounces through the halls on her way to teaching her class, in stylish dress, with impish grin, welcoming everyone. Inclusion in action.

Accessible Meetings

I recently attended a meeting at a corporate office and the person who escorted me asked: *"Would you like to take the stairs or would you rather use the elevator?"*

This simple accommodation sends a powerful message: that it's "business as usual" to acknowledge a visitor's needs and preferences.

When a meeting is being convened, at the minimum the announcement needs to provide a resource – a name and telephone number - for anyone requiring any accommodation. That way a participant knows who to go to for assistance whether for a special meal or hearing, vision, mobility or other accommodation.

Meeting planners have access to many more detailed resources. Following are some of the recommendations provided by Amy L. Allbright, Director of the American Bar Association Commission on Disability Rights:

- In choosing a venue, plan an on-site visit in advance
- Prepare a checklist of specific accessibility items, such as a barrier-free, clearly marked, well- lit accessible main entrance

- Choose meeting rooms that are well lit, have easy-to-open doors, and are large enough to allow people in wheelchairs or people with service dogs to move freely about
- In promotional and registration materials, include statements that invite people with disabilities to request accommodations.
- Work with speakers well in advance to ensure that their presentations will be accessible to everybody. For materials distributed at the meeting, offer alternative formats such as audio, electronic files, large print, or Braille.

Stephan Smith is Executive Director of AHEAD, the Association on Higher Education and Disability, which sponsors an Annual Conference attended by more than a thousand professionals involved in the development of policy and in the provision of quality services to meet the needs of people with disability involved in all areas of higher education.

Smith explains *"A significant proportion of our Conference attendees are themselves people with disability. At this conference it's very common to see service dogs and wheelchairs, scooters and sign language interpreters.*

We actually find it quite easy to accommodate everyone. Of course, we choose a facility that meets our needs, like the Sacramento Convention Center which recently hosted our group. We choose that facility in part because it was so easy for all of our participants to get in and out of and nearby hotels offered lots of accessible rooms.

We always invite our presenters to submit their materials early so that we can make the documents accessible for people who have difficulty reading.

Overall we've learned that being inclusive and welcoming is quite easy, and we are rewarded by the sense that we are on the cutting edge of inclusiveness practices."

Accessible Documents

If you're involved in creating documents for any wide audience, chances are someone in that audience will have difficulty accessing printed information.

Many people who are blind or who have low vision use screen reader software that makes on-screen information available as synthesized speech. But if there are graphics or pictures, they will be missed by the screen reader. Make the format accessible by adding text that describes the graphic. A textual description of an image, known as alternative text, will be recognized by screen readers as well as by Braille.

Screen reader software will also miss a hyperlink like www.microsoft.com but the reader will understand what to do if the reference is to "use the Microsoft website."

About 8 percent of men and 0.5 percent of women have some form of color blindness.[lvii] That means that potentially 1 in 12 readers of your document may not distinguish the colors you designed. Color blindness does not mean that people cannot see color, or that they see only in black and white. It is more that they have a reduced spectrum of colors they can distinguish between. If the graphic says "push" and shows a red button, an accessible approach will make the instruction clear through text alone.

Cognitive and language disabilities range from dyslexia to difficulties remembering, solving problems, or understanding sensory information. For people who have these disabilities, complex or inconsistent visual displays or word choices can make comprehension more difficult.

The following tips for writing documents are excellent for people with cognitive disabilities. But they are also good guidelines for writing documents for all audiences:

- Use lots of white space. Place blocks of text with white space around them. Put an extra empty line between paragraphs.
- Avoid 'busy' pages or screens. Too much going on in one page can be complicated to understand. For instance, don't

have lots of highly colored graphics, and text, and different fonts, and animations on one page.

- A bulleted or numbered list is easier to read and comprehend than a dense paragraph.

Make the text appear clear without lots of clutter. Concentrate on being precise without using complicated sentence structure. Use short sentences. All of your readers will appreciate these efforts.

Wendy Holden is responsible for student academic accommodations at Central Washington University. Wendy and others on the team have developed a product called CAR Check, an add-in for Microsoft Word for Windows which provides a centralized set of tools that assist in creating accessible documents:

This handy tool lets the writer evaluate the document with an easy to understand score card of accessibility. The CAR Checker then shows the writer how to correct issues.

Creating more accessible documents, like other inclusiveness efforts, need not be burdensome and can reap benefits far beyond the disability audience.

Hiring a Sign Language Interpreter

"Tips for Hiring Qualified Sign Language Interpreters" have been compiled by the people at deaffreindly.com. This innovative virtual organization invites reviews from the public in order to bring awareness to deaf-friendly businesses, and corrective feedback to deaf-challenged businesses. Reviewers fit a number of categories: deaf, deaf-blind, hard of hearing, friends/family of the deaf and those with a special interest in creating a deaf-friendly world.

Some of their tips for hiring an interpreter include:

- Start the hiring process as early as possible. Two weeks advance notice is the universally accepted guideline for most service providers.
- Ensure that interpreters aren't solo. Sign language interpreting can be a very physically and mentally taxing job - long hours on one's feet, constant moving of the hands, coupled with interpreting of one language to another on the fly. For jobs exceeding two hours, they say that two interpreters must be booked.
- The Registry of Interpreters for the Deaf (RID) has compiled a list encompassing the names of all nationally certified interpreters which anyone can access on their website (www.rid.org).
- Find out if the customer has a preferred interpreter. People who use interpreters frequently become very familiar with the interpreting community and their range of skill, comfort and trust.
- Remember etiquette. After a few hours on an assignment, it can be too easy to mistake a friendly interpreter as the client's "buddy." Remember that you've hired a professional who must adhere to a Professional Code of Conduct. That

means don't offer the interpreter free drinks (an interpreter must stay sober on the job). Don't ask an interpreter to do small tasks like hand out classroom papers.

- Talk to the client – not the interpreter. Look directly at the client and refrain from using phrases like "*tell her I said*" or "*what does she need?*". Do your best to speak clearly and at a medium-clip pace. Interpreters are not super-human translation devices, and are required to interrupt if what you have said is unclear.

- Create a deaf-friendly (and interpreter-friendly) environment. Many seasoned interpreters will tell you of the many interesting places their career has taken them to: Underwater for scuba diving classes, ballroom dance floors, next to hospital birthing tubs, and more. Whatever the situation, it is critical that the deaf person can see both you (speaker) and the interpreter. Take a few minutes to design your environment beforehand. Good lighting and adequate sign space is also important.

The Many Benefits of Closed Captioning

Closed captioning allows the person with a hearing disability to have access to television programming by displaying the audio portion of a television program as text on the television screen. Closed captioning provides a critical link to news, entertainment and information for individuals who are deaf or hard-of-hearing.

According to Aberdeen Broadcast Services, closed captioning benefits other people as well:

- People who are learning or improving their English language skills. In America, the number of non-native English speakers is growing and most of them are actively learning English.
- Children watching television with captions on improve their reading skills at a far faster rate than children who do not watch television with captions.
- Approximately 90 million adults measured at a relatively low level of proficiency for reading according to the National Center for Education Statistics[lviii]. Closed captioning is an effective tool for improving reading skill.

The Wonders of Universal Design

Wheelchair user John Little and his wife Suzanne designed their suburban home according to the principles of universal design. To the casual onlooker, the home seems beautiful and spacious. The houseguest notices that the shower is especially easy to get in and out of. People can work easily together in the spacious kitchen. Drawers are easy to open.

John has plenty of room to move around in his chair which can also fit well under the counters so he can enjoy cooking and preparing meals.

On a larger scale, the Ed Roberts Campus[lix] is a universally designed campus in Berkeley, CA, that brings disability services together into one building and creates a center that is a resource for everybody within the community. It is a memorial to the life of Ed Roberts who was an early leader of the independent living movement.

The campus is an excellent example of architecture with full inclusion for all people. Conceptualized over a period of 13 years, designers were able to examine how people with different disabilities use it and how people with different disabilities have differing and sometimes conflicting needs. For example, someone who is blind will appreciate a raised curb indicating entry onto the sidewalk but that same raised curb is an impediment for someone in a wheelchair.

This campus also combines Universal Design with aesthetics. Designers and architects were encouraged to look beyond code requirements as restraints but as an opportunity to be creative and to open the world for more people. The building has become an icon for the disability community, worldwide.

Dmitri Belser, Executive Director, Center for Accessible Technology at the Ed Roberts Campus offers tours to corporate people who want to integrate these principles at their facilities. He says *"This place is a mecca, and we're a portal for you."*

Following are some of the general principles of universal design along with examples that you may recognize. These principles are increasingly integrated in our architecture and public spaces.

Principles of Universal Design[ix]

- Equitable use means providing the same means of use for all users. Those automatic doors we see at shopping malls and airports are required for a person in a wheelchair, but they're also appreciated by mothers with strollers and people carrying luggage.
- Flexibility in use means a design that accommodates a wide range of individual preferences and abilities like scissors for right or left-handed users.

- Simple and intuitive use -- easy to understand, regardless of the user's experience, knowledge, language skills or current concentration level. Some instruction manuals are designed with easy to follow pictures and diagrams.
- Perceptible information that communicates necessary information regardless of the conditions of the immediate surroundings or the user's sensory abilities. As an example, important information at airports and train stations is conveyed through both printed signage and voice announcements.

- Tolerance for error, meaning that the design minimizes hazards and adverse consequences of accidental or unintended actions.

Forgiving. An example is the "undo" feature in computer software that allows the user to correct mistakes.

- Low physical effort which can be used efficiently and comfortably like levered handles on doors that can be opened easily, even by someone with an armload of packages.

- Size and space for approach and use regardless of the user's body size, posture or mobility, for example the wide gates at subway stations designed to accommodate all users.

The Welcoming Handshake

In concluding our chapter on creating a welcoming environment we invite you to think about that ubiquitous gesture of welcome, the handshake. In our traditional welcome, we extend the hand. But sometimes we may hesitate.

Let's have a look at what might cause that momentary hesitation.

The person with a Parkinson's tremor may seem too fragile. Or we may not know exactly how to manage the handshake with the person who is blind. Or if someone has a hand prosthesis we may be discomfited. *"What's the right thing to do?"* we may wonder.

> *"I dread handshakes. I've got some problems with my hands, and everywhere I go, people want to impress me with their grip."*
>
> George Forman
> 2 X World Heavyweight Champion

To be truly welcoming, always offer to shake hands. If someone's hands seem fragile due to arthritis or a neurological condition, be gentle. And resist the inclination to be unnecessarily firm in your grip.

If you're greeting a person who is blind you can say: *"May I shake your hand?"* Chances are, he'll offer his. You might then extend the welcome by offering a place to sit -- tap the seat -- and a place to set his belongings…. *"There's a table to your left if you'd like to put your briefcase there."*

A person who is deaf or hard of hearing may not realize that you're about to offer your hand. Gain her attention with eye contact or with a light tap. Too often our deaf colleagues complain about being handled roughly when someone tries to gain their attention.

If someone has a hand prosthetic, extend yours along with a welcoming smile. The merest touch will complete this important gesture and will create the potential for you to feel connected.

Perhaps you're visiting a family whose grown son has Down syndrome. You may shake hands with the parents and find that the son throws his arms around you in an exuberant hug! Depending on your own comfort level you can return the hug, or draw back and say something like *"It's quite a surprise to get such a greeting! Let's shake hands."*

In that moment when the welcoming handshake is called for, notice any hesitation and know that you can take a breath and then step into a hospitable greeting even if the circumstances are somewhat unfamiliar.

This chapter may have awakened your attention on how to be more welcoming in a variety of situations. The conversation about creating a more inclusive world may begin by talking freely about disability, yet the benefits of the inquiry can inform many areas of our lives.

ANXIETY, PITY AND OTHER UNCOMFORTABLE FEELINGS

"Feelings will always be a part of your work. The more you try to squash them the more control those feelings will have."

Law & Order Special Victim's Unit,

Captain Cragen to Detective Stabler

We are one diagnosis away from being blinded or made deaf. We are one car accident away from losing our legs. We are one stroke away from losing language or our ability to organize our thoughts. Depressing? Well, yes, that loss could cause depression, sadness, rage - all of the uncomfortable feelings that life's losses can bring. The loss of a job, a marriage, an untimely death, loss of savings, loss of face, loss of expectations when a child is born with a disability or when a couple can't conceive the baby they desperately want. But because of the way we are constructed as human beings, most of us usually pass through and survive the period of loss. We can be happy again, hopeful again, productive again.

You can project your feelings and fears onto the person who is deaf or blind or has another disability. But it remains your fear, your projection and it can prevent the possibility of a real relationship.

When I speak publicly about people with disabilities, as soon as I describe a person who has one of these or other issues going on I am met with voluble gasps of sympathy and sighs of pity from the audience. Those uncomfortable reactions surface immediately. Let's challenge ourselves to move out of the shadows of these feelings and into a brighter clearing where the possibility for a new and genuine relationship is possible. There is so much to be gained.

A Word about Odd or Unsettling Behavior

"We have a customer who comes in from time to time who talks in circles, blanks out and gets very negative....do you have any advice for how to serve that customer or others like him?"

Questions like this are frequently raised when we work with groups who serve the public. From time to time we're bound to encounter a person who exhibits odd, unsettling or even scary behavior. And with the long term difficulties with employment, people's behavior may be even more edgy than usual. What causes this behavior and what can we can we do in response?

Causes

Let's think of various adjectives to describe what we're discussing here – essentially, behavior that may strike us as odd, unsettling, scary, weird, or bizarre. When we have no context for evaluating what's up with the person, we have no way of knowing what's causing it. Any number of possibilities could come into play:

- She could be a person diagnosed with a mental illness like schizophrenia or bipolar disorder who is "off her meds" (that is, who has stopped taking medication which controls her behavior so it falls within customary social bounds).

- He could be a person with impulse control issues that make it hard for him to adhere to typical social standards. Poor impulse control can be a symptom of Tourette's Syndrome (characterized, among other things, by unusual vocalizations), traumatic brain injury, Autism, Asperger's Syndrome, or other cognitive disorders.

- She could be on stress overload, without any particular diagnosis but at an exceedingly difficult time in her life due to relationship problems or divorce, illness in the family or economic distress. She could be temporarily "crazy".

Those of us who work with the public may not be in a position to know much, if anything, about the cause of a person's odd or unsettling behavior - but we nonetheless need to perform our jobs.

Responses

We'll focus on four things to think about. First, we'll emphasize the importance of safety and being ready and able to initiate a safety plan. Secondly we'll talk about framing the desired outcome of the interaction. Third, we'll discuss the importance of limiting or setting boundaries around our own expectations about the outcome, and finally we'll discuss next steps – what to do when the person leaves.

Safety First

If your job involves working in a public setting where anyone from the community can approach you, you should have guidelines in place for your own protection and the protection of others in your workplace. There is always a possibility, however remote, that you will be endangered by someone around you. If your workplace doesn't have a safety plan, take the initiative to see that you get one.

Your safety plan may include access to an alarm and easy access to a phone. You must not put yourself in a position where you are with people you don't know behind closed doors or in isolated or remote areas.

How do you know when to get help? Well, you don't know for certain. But there are signs you should get help: if you see a weapon; if the person touches you; if you feel afraid. These three cases represent a continuum with the first case, the seen weapon, as the most urgent and the third case, feeling afraid, the most ambiguous or uncertain as to whether reaching out for help is the right thing to do.

Some people have told us that they actually say: "*You're scaring me.*" In most instances the person will immediately tone down his behavior which was simply the result of intense emotion and unintentional.

It is your obligation to protect yourself and the other people in your workplace if you believe you are in harm's way by following your workplace safety plan.

Frame the Outcome

If a person is behaving in an odd or unsettling manner, it's important for you to make up your mind on what you want the outcome to be.

If you are in a mall parking lot and someone nearby is behaving in a way that alarms you, stay very focused on what your desired outcome is. You want to get into the car and go home. Stay focused on that. If you are a service representative at a bank, you will want the customer to complete her transaction. Communicate with the person in a clear and calm manner so that you achieve your desired outcome.

Set Boundaries About the Outcome

At some point, you may find that your internal alarm escalates. If you are in the mall parking lot and find that the individual who is scaring you now interferes with your ability to get into your car and leave, you're in trouble. Throw your keys away and run. Or yell for help. Or get into the car if you can and lock the doors. Protect yourself. Know when to be afraid.

Next Steps

After a scary incident has occurred, it's important to decide what to do next. You have an obligation to protect yourself and others from an individual who has been that frightening. On the other hand, if you over reacted to someone's bad temper it's important to recognize your own vulnerability.

Definitive advice is beyond the scope of this book but it's worth saying: think about what to do when confronted with a person whose behavior is odd or unsettling. Stay conscious and alert to your inner voice. Err on the side of getting help or support. An excellent resource is <u>The Gift of Fear</u> by Gavin de Becker[lxi]. The author does a great job of helping us articulate when to be afraid and when not to be afraid, and what to do in either event. Local law enforcement and workplace providers in human resources and EAPs (employee assistance plans) may also offer useful guidelines.

If you are in a situation that is frightening, pay attention and make some mature decisions. Don't find yourself in serious trouble afterwards, and wish you had paid attention earlier.

CONCLUSION

If you're reading this page you've probably read the whole book which is an accomplishment in itself, in these busy times with so many distractions.

But something about this book makes it a particular accomplishment because it means you're able to sit still through the dark parts. Parts of this book are dark, no doubt.

But those of us who are committed to living a full life know that taking on the dark parts is part of life. And the ability to do that liberates us for the joyous parts.

Many thanks for your time and attention.

The book opened with a quote from the Talmud, and closes with another:

It is not upon you to finish the job, nor are you to desist from it.[lxii]

Take on the job of full inclusion. You don't have to finish it.

Linda Fitzpatrick

♿ Disability Inclusion - Seven Themes

1. Ask before helping.
2. Maintain eye contact.
3. Don't Shout.
4. Avoid outdated language.
5. Don't worry about reminding someone of their disability.
6. Don't pretend to understand if you don't.
7. See the person first, not the disability.

FOR MORE INFORMATION ABOUT LINDA FITZPATRICK AND HER WORK VISIT WWW.WORKTHATSATISFIES.COM

RESOURCES

Patience is not a virtue - it's a necessity, a survival trait.

Terry Anderson, <u>Den of Lions</u>

The disability community is large, diverse and constantly growing and changing. Whatever you might need help with, chances are it exists. You'll just have to spend some time to find exactly what you need. For basic internet searches, simply type your questions or key words into your favorite search engine. It's a place to start.

Another powerful resource is LinkedIn (www.linkedin.com). Look for groups of people who may share your issues or have particular skill or knowledge in that area. Type in key words and see what groups come up. Then go visit, virtually (that is online), and ask people there to help you.

On the following pages there are a few ideas to get you started but this list is far from comprehensive.

Trust that you can find the assistance you need with just a little tenacity…and patience helps, too.

National Organization on Disability (www.nod.org)

This is a cross-disability resource with a special emphasis on employment opportunities for people with disabilities.

Job Accommodation Network (www.askjan.org)

Provides assistance on workplace accommodations or the Americans with Disabilities Act (ADA) for individuals and businesses.

ADA.gov

This comprehensive website provides technical assistance publications on a wide array of topics from general questions and answers to very specific issues (like accessibility requirements for swimming pools).

Illustrated Guide to Assistive Technology and Devices: Tools and Gadgets for Living Independently by Suzanne Robitaille

A comprehensive book published by Demos Health

AbledBody: Where can-do is done different

This vibrant online resource is a news and media platform for families touched by physical or mental disability, and those who engage with the disability community.

Disability Advocates – LinkedIn Online Group

Log onto LinkedIn.com to see the conversations in this vibrant online group which has thousands of members. Post your questions and contribute to others.

Society for Accessible Travel and Hospitality (www.sath.org)

Members of this organization include travel professionals, consumers with disability and other individuals and organizations who support accessible travel.

US Business Leadership Network (www.USBLN.org)

According to its website "The US Business Leadership Network® (USBLN®) is a national non-profit that helps business drive performance by leveraging disability inclusion in the workplace, supply chain, and marketplace". Also offers Disability-Owned Business Enterprise Certification to help corporate members expand their diversity programs.

U.S. Department of Justice

For more information about the revised ADA regulations and 2010 ADA Standards, please visit the Department of Justice's ADA Website or call the toll-free number.

ADA Website
http://www.ADA.gov/

ADA Information Line
800-514-0301 (Voice)
800-514-0383 (TTY)

24 hours a day to order publications by mail.
M-W, F 9:30 a.m. 5:30 p.m., Th 12:30 p.m. 5:30 p.m. (Eastern Time) to speak to an ADA Specialist. All calls are confidential.

ADA National Network (DBTAC)

Ten regional centers are funded by the U.S. Department of Education to provide ADA technical assistance to businesses, States and localities, and persons with disabilities. One toll-free number connects you to the center in your region:

800-949-4232 (Voice and TTY)
http://www.adata.org/

Access Board

For technical assistance on the ADA/ABA Accessibility Guidelines:

800-872-2253 (Voice)
800-992 -2822 (TTY)

Changing Paces

A Canadian firm specializing in legislative compliance programs, disability inclusion coaching, and inspiring motivational speaking by Principal Trish Robichaud.

info@changingpaces.com
905-967-3014

Internal Revenue Service

For information on the Disabled Access Tax Credit (Form 8826) and the Section 190 tax deduction (Publication 535 Business Expenses):

800-829-3676 (Voice) or 800-829-4059 (TTY)
http://www.irs.gov/

REFERENCES

[i] ADA reference that we choose to use

[ii] http://www.eeoc.gov/laws/statutes/adaaa.cfm

[iii] Figure 1 US Census

[iv] My Beloved World by Sonia Sotomayor, Knopf Doubleday Publishing Group 1/15/2013

[v] http://www.washingtonpost.com/opinions/living-well-with-down-syndrome/2012/05/01/gIQAZqrExT_gallery.html#photo=1?

[vi] http://www.census.gov/prod/2008pubs/p70-117.pdf

[vii] My Stroke of Insight: A Brain Scientist's Personal Journey, Jill Bolte Taylor, Penguin Group USA, 2008

[viii] The Question of David: A Disabled Mother's Journey Through Adoption, Family and Life by Denise Sherer Jacobson, CreateSpace Independent Publishing Platform (February 1, 1999)

[ix] http://affluent.net/sara/

[x] http://livingwithcfs.com/blog/

[xi] Invisible Wounds: Mental Health and Cognitive Care Needs of America's Returning Veterans (Rand Institute July 2013 Research Briefs RB-9336)

[xii] From Bipolar Darkness, The Empathy to Be a Doctor March 17, 2009, The New York Times

[xiii] You can learn more about John's story at: http

[xiv] For more examples of People First Language visit

http://nti.unc.edu/healthy_inclusion/downloads/People%20First%20Chart.pdf

xv Freeman, Michael (2002). Human rights: an interdisciplinary approach. Cambridge: Polity Press

xvii http://www.ada.gov/olmstead/olmstead_about.htm

xviii http://www2.ed.gov/programs/atsg/index.html

xix http://idea.ed.gov/

xx NY Times Giving Mobility When Legs Can't (September 8, 2013)

xxi DisabilityLand by Alan Brightman, SelectBooks (March 1, 2008)

xxii The Illustrated Guide to Assistive Technology and Devices: Tools and Gadgets for Living Independently by Suzanne Robitaille Publisher: Demos Health; 1 edition (December 8, 2009)

xxiii http://www.nytimes.com/2013/04/18/us/war-and-sports-shape-better-artificial-limbs.html

xxiv When Cancer Comes Back: Cancer Recurrence, American Cancer Society, 05/13/2013

xxv CDC Fast Facts: HIV in the United States

xxvi http://www.bls.gov/news.release/pdf/disabl.pdf
xxvii April 2008 HR Magazine

xxviii Photo of physician http://images-cdn.lancasteronline.com/25208_640.jpg

xxix http://askjan.org/ERguide/ERGuide.pdf

xxx US Department of Labor – ODEP – Office of Disability

xxxi http://www.gallup.com/poll/163619/depression-costs-workplaces-billion-absenteeism.aspx

xxxii

http://www.cdc.gov/workplacehealthpromotion/implementation/topics/depression.html

xxxiii
http://images.forbes.com/forbesinsights/StudyPDFs/Innovation_Through_Diversity.pdf

xxxiv http://www.hrmagazine.co.uk/hr/features/1145395/randy-lewis-havent-disability-employ

xxxv Photo charsheeh@aol.com inset Walgreen's staff

http://www.asse.org/professionalsafety/pastissues/057/06/062_071_F1Ka_0612.pdf

xxxvi

http://www.kter.org/conference/materials/docs/SafetyManagement.pdf

xxxvii

http://www.fastcompany.com/welcome.html?destination=http://www.fastcompany.com/3002957/disabled-employee-amendment

xxxviii http://www.nytimes.com/2014/10/05/us/a-couple-gaining-independence-and-finding-a-bond.html?_r=0

xxxix http://www.disabilityscoop.com/2014/03/25/feds-disability-hiring-mandate/19222/

[i] http://www.disabilityscoop.com/2014/03/25/feds-disability-hiring-mandate/19222/

xl

xli 2014 AHEAD/Pepnet2 Conference in Sacramento: Growing new Skill and Enthusiasm for your Career by Linda Fitzpatrick

xlii http://www.viscardicenter.org/stories/meet-richard.html

xliii http://www.successfulresumes.com.au/

xliv http://www.and.org.au/

xlv http://www.cbc.ca/m/news/business/big-business-how-disabilities-are-transforming-the-marketplace-1.2764814

xlvi Society for Human Resource Management: The Business Case: Why Diversity and Inclusion
are Good for Business

xlvii
http://www.shrm.org/hrdisciplines/Diversity/Articles/Pages/BusinessesTargetCustomers.aspx

xlviii http://www.linkedin.com/pub/greg-hale/8/502/313

xlix Note all of these references – through to McDonalds – came from the above SHRM article

l http://www.katenashassociates.com/sites/default/files/Disability-Affinity-Groups-Rudney_JBC1.pdf

li http://jenniferbrownconsulting.com/site/wp-content/uploads/2010/11/Disability-Affinity-Groups-Rudney_JBC.pdf

lii http://www.sbecouncil.org/about-us/facts-and-data/

liii http://www.ada.gov/smbusgd.pdf

liv http://brailleworks.com/applebees-braille-menus-now-available/

lv http://www.asha.org/Aud/Articles/Untreated-Hearing-Loss-in-Adults/

lvi http://www.ada.gov/pubs/mythfct.txt

lvii http://office.microsoft.com/en-us/frontpage-help/create-an-accessible-office-document-RZ006380094.aspx?section=4

lviii https://nces.ed.gov/pubs93/93275.pdf

lix http://www.universaldesign.com/about-universal-design/499-news-and-media/262-ed-roberts-campus-building-community.html

lx NC State University Center for Universal Design, College of Design.

lxi The Gift of Fear: Survival Signals That Protect Us from Violence, Gavin de Becker, Random House Publishing,

lxii https://www.jewishvirtuallibrary.org/jsource/Judaism/pirkei_avot.html